Towers
of
Hope

"There are many broken and hurting people in the world, and we are part of that wounded humanity yearning for healing and wholeness. Joy Carol tells so eloquently these moving stories that fill us with hope that we too can become more whole, more who we have it in us to become, all of what God intended us to be."

—**Archbishop Desmond Tutu**

"Joy Carol has given us a book about hope — real reasons to have it, based on lived experience and documented cases of healings. Without the ground of hope, we lose the basis for action. Without hope, we fall into cynicism and despair. Hope is inextricably tied to humility and wonder, acceptance of the fact that we don't know all the answers. Carol's lovingly crafted, wide-ranging stories of healing and recovery give a strong testimony to what some might call the miraculous. She makes hope logical and reasonable."

—**China Galland**, author, *The Bond Between Women: A Journey to Fierce Compassion* and *Longing for Darkness: Tara and the Black Madonna*

"At this time, two compelling subjects are being discussed: the serious need for healing and the power of our stories. We can read book after book on theory and formulas about healing, but in the end, it is the human story that speaks to us. Joy Carol has combined the subject of healing with the power of personal story in a way that inspires the reader toward their own potential. We are impressed with the passion and insight with which she has made these stories come to life."

—**Harville Hendrix** and **Helen LaKelly Hunt**, authors,
Getting the Love You Want and *Keeping the Love You Find*

"Joy Carol's book makes an important contribution to the growing awareness of healing as a human task and opportunity. These stories illustrate healing as many-faceted, from personal experiences to efforts to make whole our body politic and our life on the planet. This collection has much to offer everyone, from social change activists to people struggling with their own and their family's needs for healing."

—**Mary Zepernick**, author and former U.S. President of
the Women's International League for Peace and Freedom

"In earliest times, the survival of a tribe often depended upon its storytelling. People sat around campfires and heard the stories of how others had met great challenges and persevered. What was true for our ancestors is true for us today. We need to hear stories of personal triumph and transformation through difficulties — like the powerful and touching ones Joy Carol has collected in this book. As dramatic as these stories are, they are also full of concrete ideas that all of us can use to find healing opportunities in our own lives. Carol's masterful framing of these universal teachings makes the book an accessible and very useful resource for healing groups and study circles."

—**Frederic and Mary Ann Brussat**, coauthors, *Spiritual Literacy* and *Spiritual Rx*

"It is very helpful to read about the lives of individuals confronting tragedy and how they have coped and healed. They show us how the unthinkable is possible — that in the suffering of the world, reconciliation can be found. Joy Carol shows us how to use these experiences as preparation for our own healing."

—**Don Watson**, author, *Energy Conservation* and *Climatic Design*

"It is in telling our stories that healing of many kinds happens, and some stories bring the gift of healing to all who read them. Somehow, through grace, presence, and a keen listening ear and heart, Joy Carol has gathered a remarkable collection of important stories of healing that speak to both our individual lives and our collective search for hope and meaning. Always an important topic, this unique book now takes on an urgency and an immediateness that will be a gift to all who read it. It is a celebration of mystery and new life, beautifully conveyed."

—**Nina H. Frost**, Principal of The Vocare Group, author, *Soul Mapping: An Imaginative Way to Self-Discovery*

"The documented story of a Mi'kmaq, who suffered the loss of his culture and identity and who sank into alcohol and drug abuse, and his tough road to repossess his life and cultural integrity, has never been told. The telling of this story in Joy Carol's book forms part of the healing process."

—**Chief Mickey Augustine**, Mi'kmaq First Nation

Towers of Hope

Stories to Help Us Heal

Joy Carol

FOREST OF PEACE
Publishing

Suppliers for the Spiritual Pilgrim
Leavenworth, KS

Towers of Hope

copyright © 2002, by Joy Carol

Library of Congress Cataloging-in-Publication Data

Due to events surrounding September 11, 2001, and subsequent interruptions in U.S. mail delivery and government operations, this data was not yet available at the time of publication. The Cataloging-in-Publication Data for this title may be viewed by searching on the Library of Congress CIP Web site.

published by
Forest of Peace Publishing, Inc.
PO Box 269
Leavenworth, KS 66048-0269   USA
1-800-659-3227
www.forestofpeace.com

printed by
Hall Commercial Printing
Topeka, KS 66608-0007

1st printing: January 2002

Dedication

This book is lovingly dedicated to:

Alma Johanna and Wilson Julius Haupt,
my beloved parents,
and to all my family.

They are truly Towers of Hope.

Acknowledgments and Gratitude for Healing Hope

This has been a much-blessed book — a truly healing Tower of Hope. Behind this book are many people who have helped to turn my dream of a book of healing stories into a reality. I thank each and every one of you, for I have no greater gift than the hope and support you have given me.

Over the last two years as I was writing the book, my parents, Alma and Wilson Haupt, always checked on its progress. "How is your book coming along?" they would ask. "When will it be done?" By gently questioning and "pushing" me, I felt encouraged to keep working on it, even during times when I felt bogged down. Mother and Daddy were elated when they learned the book would be published. When I was visiting my family in California just days before my mother had a massive stroke, I showed her a photocopy of the attractive cover. I'll always remember and treasure the way her face lit up as she looked at it. One week later, on November 26, 2001, my beautiful mother peacefully departed this earth. I have deep gratitude for my parents' endless hopefulness, and for their trust and belief in me and in this book.

As my family helped my mother go through her transition from this earthly life, the extraordinary people at Forest of Peace Publishing were "pushing" to "birth" Towers of Hope as quickly as possible. They first received the manuscript in late October 2001. Working diligently and skillfully, they miraculously edited and published the book in time for the Holy Days at the end of the year. I am so grateful for the extraordinary leadership and support of Tom Turkle, the publisher, and for the unfaltering support and insights from my editor, Tom Skorupa — precious gifts of hope.

There are many more towers of hope for which I'm deeply grateful: the courageous and inspiring people who openly shared their healing stories and who have showed us how to live with joy and hope even in the midst of suffering and tears; my "big sis" Shirley, whom I appreciate more than she will ever know for always being there for me at the right moment and for giving the book its special title; my neurosurgeon and friend, Dr. Harold F. Young, Chief Neurosurgeon at the Medical Colleges of Virginia Hospitals, who filled me with hope as I faced my brain tumor and who challenged me to be involved in my own "healing"; my friends Mary Ann and Frederic Brussat, who offered me some much-appreciated and helpful editorial suggestions and who introduced me to Forest of Peace Publishing; my pal Gab McDonough, who lovingly read every word of every chapter at least several times; my guardian angel Rosemary Weintraub, who continues to watch over me; my friends Helen LaKelly Hunt and Harville Hendrix, who showed endless enthusiasm for my book; Ned Leavitt, who gave me good advice along the way; and Susanne Wey, who translated some of Anna's chapter.

Table of Contents

Help us to be the always hopeful
Gardeners of the Spirit
Who know that without darkness
Nothing comes to birth
As without light
Nothing flowers.

– May Sarton

Introduction

It is by going down into the abyss
that we recover the treasures of life.

– Joseph Campbell

On September 11, 2001, life seemed to stop when terrorists brutally attacked the World Trade Center and the Pentagon. In New York City, it was a terrible time: Thousands of people missing and assumed dead, hundreds of firemen and policemen killed, the tall Twin Towers of the World Trade Center demolished into a pile of ashes and debris, communications and transportation shut down, our country invaded and violated. Suddenly there was a gaping wound in our existence — raw, frightening, sad, unknown, seemingly without hope.

It was a gorgeous day, primary election day in New York City. I had voted early that morning and was traveling downtown on a Number Nine subway train. At Times Square, we heard the announcement "No more subway service." No reason given. Emerging from the underground tunnels into the brilliant sunlight of that almost-perfect day, I found myself in the middle of thousands of tourists and New Yorkers staring at the huge electronic television screens in Times Square. There, locked in utter disbelief and shock, we stood watching the outrageous destruction of the Twin Towers, those sleek and proud symbols of freedom and hope, as they crumbled in slow-motion, taking with them thousands of lives and hopes and dreams. There was a blood-chilling fear in the air when we learned that terrorists had hijacked commercial airplanes with innocent passengers on board and had intentionally crashed them into the outlandishly vulnerable Twin Towers. As messages about businesses closing flashed across the bottom of the screen, I thought: "This isn't really happening; this is not real." Eventually the horrified crowds began to leave the area to return to their hotels or their homes in Manhattan, Brooklyn, Queens, the Bronx, Upstate New York, Connecticut, New Jersey.

Then began what felt like the saddest and longest journey of silence and fear. Millions of numbed people slowly moved en masse through the streets of Manhattan past frantic people in phone booths trying to call someone, past the darkened theatre district and Lincoln Center, past silenced schools and universities, closed banks and shops. A few shoe stores handed out sneakers to women limping home in high-heeled shoes and business suits. Some people began to panic as we walked. Perhaps we were really at war. Long lines formed at ATM machines as people worried that cash would run out. Many grocery stores were closed, and those that remained open tried to deal with people desperately trying to buy food and bottled water. Maybe the water system had been poisoned or contaminated.

As I walked the miles I had an almost frantic need to reach someone I loved — my parents, my sister, my niece, a friend. I wanted to tell everyone I knew that I was alive, to tell them what had happened. But phone lines and circuits were damaged or heavily used and it wasn't possible to contact anyone.

It's hard to describe the devastation, pain and sorrow people felt in the great city as we moved through the streets that day to our homes where we glued ourselves in front of television sets and radios to hear the latest news and lick our wounds. What had happened was tragic, unbelievable, and we were shattered and immensely sad.

For a few days we only moved around the city with a great deal of effort due to limited subway service, entire sections of the city being closed and no traffic in tunnels or on key bridges. It was possible to leave Manhattan, but you might not be able to return. We walked long distances to get to work, to buy groceries, to see a friend.

Like many concerned New Yorkers, I wanted to help others who were in need of healing. So I volunteered as a grief counselor and spiritual director in the Armory Crisis Center on Lexington Avenue, trying to help families deal with their loss and grief as they continued to search for their missing loved ones. They told me hundreds of stories of suffering, loss, bravery, compassion and hope. I will always remember the faces and stories of security guards, waiters, firemen, out-of-town guests, financial advisors, people who had gone in early to cover for colleagues, missing children, missing couples, children who still left messages on their missing parents' cell phones.

Although I felt crushed with fatigue as I left the Armory each day, I also had a glimmer of hope from the stories I heard. Certainly life in New York City and in our country and the world had changed. We would likely never be quite the same. Not necessarily worse or better, but very different. It felt like years had passed since we had lived what seemed a "normal life" — before the attack on the Twin Towers, before the ashes and smoke, anger and sadness, incredible bravery and compassion, the National Guard, jet fighter planes overhead, and a great hole in our hearts and in the skyline of our much-loved Manhattan.

By the fifth day, I experienced my own meltdown when I stood in tears at a fruit stand unable to make a decision about which fruit to buy. The understanding man who gave me an apple must have been an angel. I was exhausted and overwhelmed with the ever-present bombardment of devastating news and neediness, the feeling of isolation, the unbelievable sense of loss, the constant smell of smoke in the air — even in my uptown apartment. I knew it was essential to take time out, to get perspective, to do some healing work for myself. When I called my sister, I broke down completely and sobbed like a baby. She listened to me tell my stories of sadness and of hope — just what I needed.

Each of the persons I talk with feels a sense of pain and loss following the traumatic terrorist attacks on September 11, 2001. They too want to tell their stories of sorrow, of courage, of compassion. As I have listened to people around the country and the world, I have learned that each one of us is in need of hope and "healing."

Don't you go letting life harden your heart...we can let the circumstances of our lives harden us so that we become increasingly resentful or afraid, or we can let them soften us and make us kinder. We always have the choice.

– The Dalai Lama

Over the last decades, life has felt extremely fast-paced, competitive, impersonal, violent and stressful. The threat of terrorism has also forced people around the world to live with the fear of hijackings, bomb threats, even war. The world seems out of control. Personal and collective traumas cause us to feel off balance, to want to withdraw or go into hiding. Almost everything and everybody can be viewed as some kind of enemy to do battle with or as a threat to be avoided.

If we become accustomed to this way of living, we may have difficulty making changes because we are filled with anxiety and fear. If we hang on to old emotional, social or political wounds, we may continue to reinjure ourselves and live with a very limited sense of self. Especially during times of severe crises we can feel damaged, hopeless, forsaken and in the dark of our lives, without a clue about how we might be "healed."

About six years ago, I faced three close encounters with death in three years: a lethal streptococcus infection, a serious accident as a pedestrian hit by a car and a brain tumor. During those traumatic, frightening times, I learned that I needed a lot of "healing" beyond my obvious physical needs. I came to value how precious it is to be alive, to have the opportunity to wake up to a new day. I also realized that we can appreciate and celebrate life even though we may not have what we want, or do what we want or be able to "fix" what goes wrong in our lives.

My life-threatening experiences taught me that we can "heal" and live life fully, even when we are in the abyss of suffering. In discussions with others, I discovered that many people have had similar experiences of "healing." They too have learned that it is possible to have peace of mind and a better, more whole way of living.

Although we may be unable to change the terrible things that happen to us, we *are* able to change how we respond to them. We can transform what seems like a hopeless situation into a personal triumph, and we can experience "healing." We may even find wholeness in our losses, traumas, disabilities and failures.

By "healing," I do not mean "curing," which is a narrow concept usually associated with the restoration of physical health. Curing is still the main focus of the Western health care system, involving the skilled use of diagnostic tools; technological, surgical and chemical interventions; and the authority of experts to mount a concentrated assault on broken body parts. Curing implies that the person who receives a treatment is passive and the one who offers it is active. In far too many cases, the patient is regarded as the victim of disease who should submit to knowledgeable powers of the medical establishment.

Healing may involve curing, but it should not be limited to that outcome. Nor should it be reduced to images of evangelists and faith healers promising miracles or practitioners of a variety of alternative modes of treatment. I believe everyone would benefit if we redefined and expanded the concept of healing.

In this book are the stories of people who experienced challenging life-damaging or life-threatening situations and who suffered emotionally, spiritually, physically, socially and politically. They responded to their dilemmas by choosing to change radically and positively the picture for themselves as well as for many around them. Each one found some kind of "healing." Not one of them was totally cured, nor did they have that expectation.

Their stories range geographically from South Africa to Vietnam, Northern Ireland, Canada, Harlem, California and elsewhere. Their need for healing emanated from a wide variety of difficulties, some intensely personal, others reflective of major problems in our world. Although deeply wounded from life-threatening illnesses, physical disabilities, mental and physical abuse, discrimination, torture, addictions, imprisonment, war and approaching death, these people chose not to allow their woundedness to define who they were. Instead of feeling damaged, they openly and courageously faced their injuries and concerns and reacted positively to them. They used a variety of methods in their healing process to make their disabilities and adversities empowering rather than incapacitating. Some ended up viewing their problems as gifts.

If there is a single definition of healing it is to enter with mercy and awareness those pains, mental and physical, from which we have withdrawn in judgment and dismay.

– Stephen Levine

Every one of these stories is filled with remarkable lessons. As I interviewed these people, I discovered how far-reaching and expansive the concept of healing can be. My earlier, more traditional definition of healing has since yielded to a broader and more comprehensive one. Here are elements I now include in my definition of healing.

Healing Is:

- **Becoming whole.** It is a lifelong journey of becoming fully human. It involves the totality of our being: body, mind, emotion, spirit, social and political context, as well as our relationships with others and with the Divine. Healing does not necessarily mean being happy or getting what we think we want out of life. Becoming whole means growth, often with some pain.

- **Becoming our authentic self.** The healing process involves releasing old self-images that may not be genuine and discovering who and what we really are, not what we think we should be. Healing is knowing why we are here and what we really value. It restores our ability to hear and heed our dreams and aspirations.

- **Reconnecting lost aspects of our selves,** paying attention to buried feelings and to places inside us that are distressed, unhappy or always sick. It enables us to express our self in its fullness, both the light and the shadow sides.

- **Being open to change and new possibilities** not considered before, responding to problems and dilemmas by changing the picture. It means being willing to let in more of life, to open up to what may have been previously closed or destroyed for us and yet which holds promise of giving us new life, new pleasure and new fulfillment.

- **Facing our fears and refusing to be injured or wounded,** which may require changing our belief systems, breaking taboos, letting go of what is familiar and stepping into the unknown.

- **Accepting that problems, pain, and suffering are part of life** and inseparable from us — not a peripheral relationship, not something isolated or avoidable. This acceptance enables us to enter into problems and use suffering, pain and life-threatening events to enrich our lives.

- **Being empowered** by the Divine and by others. Through the discovery of meaning in our defects, disorders, problems and diseases, we may experience new degrees of creativity and life forces that we might never have seen or imagined before our difficulty. We may find that our pains and fears are transformed into relief and confidence.

- **Recognizing the value and preciousness of life,** knowing that every moment is unique and significant. This realization usually leads to a greater appreciation of the wonder of our minds, bodies and spirits and of the Divine.

- **Having faith and hope,** which are two of the important preconditions for mental and physical health. Faith and hope — a belief in the Divine, the meaning of human life and the universe — help us to claim our capacity to create and make something new.

- **Finding inner peace,** contentment and tranquility amid the realities of our daily life, including its problems, changes and chaos. Often this involves experiencing a sense of fullness that makes the burdens of pain or illness lighter.

- **Being forgiving of our self and others and being forgiven;** giving our self and others the freedom to let go of rivalry, strife, anger, hatred, fear and limitations.

- **Feeling connected to one another** and a sense of interdependence, knowing we are not isolated or autonomous, giving up the illusions of boundaries in life. This attitude, in turn, leads to taking responsibility, acting justly and accepting that we share our humanity with each other.

- **Being loving and loved,** having a feeling of loving one's self and wanting to love and serve others, as well as being capable of receiving love. With loving comes an ability to trust, a feeling of aliveness and a sense of greater participation in life.

Healing is a lifelong journey toward wholeness.

– Jeanne Achterberg

Since ancient times, storytelling has been used as a beneficial and powerful tool in the healing process. To tell our story, to be heard, is strong medicine. Healing stories can touch our hearts and tear away some of our illusions. They can help us understand that life is a series of challenges — not all good, not all bad. We may even be able to experience our own lives and the world in new ways. Healing stories can help us expand our consciousness to see our lives and the world in new ways.

Our reading of the moving accounts and challenges the people in this book faced helps us put our own wounds, fears and difficulties in a meaningful and hopeful context. By sharing their choices and movements toward healing and wholeness, they become companions and guides showing us how we can achieve our own transitions from pain and suffering toward joy and fulfillment. Through them we understand more about both living and dying. Their stories have the power to reach out to us and have a healing effect on us.

Every one of these stories contains powerful lessons that can speak to our needs for healing in the present difficult situations in which we live. This is a time of fear, insecurity, change and uncertainty. The people who tell these stories have faced similar, often greater, problems and have found healing.

As you read this book, I encourage you to think of ways that you and others have been healed. I also invite you to expand your ideas about healing and to recognize and celebrate the choices you have made and the healing you have already done in your own life by seeing it mirrored in the healing stories of others. It is my hope that you will also learn some strategies for the healing you have yet to do for yourself, your life and the world.

All of the stories in this book show us that there is good news in the midst of suffering, that people are resilient, that they have a desire to heal. They stand like strong saplings reaching for the sky with optimism and perseverance to recover the treasures of life. They are truly Towers of Hope.

Because there are seeds of healing and hope in the ashes of the Twin Towers of the World Trade Center, I begin with two short stories of healing related to that tragedy.

Where there is ruin,
there is a hope for treasure.

– Rumi

Hope stretches the limits of what is possible.
It is linked with that basic trust in life
without which we could not
get from one day to the next.

– Mary C. Grey

MAUREEN AND DANNY

Towers of Compassion

I know Danny would want us to think about what we should do —
not to retaliate in rage, but to respond in a way
that will make this world a better place for everyone.
— Maureen

Her face had a look of tranquility as she walked toward me at the Crisis Center in the Armory. On my table was the latest list of the survivors who had been hospitalized since the September 11th tragedy at the Twin Towers. It was the last stop at the Center in a long process of registering the missing persons. At first it seemed this calm woman was not a family member of one of the missing victims. She didn't show any signs of shock, denial, anger or grief.

She took my extended hand in her warm hands, and our eyes connected for a few seconds. She simply said, "My name is Maureen. My brother Danny is missing."

"Would you like to tell me about your brother?" I asked. As she lifted her eyes from the thick stack of papers containing nearly 6,000 names, a gentle smile came across her face. "I can't think of anything I'd rather do," she replied.

Maureen and Danny

Danny was just turning 30 this week. We were planning a big surprise party for him this weekend. Seven of his cousins and buddies were coming to New York City from different parts of the country to celebrate the day with him. Everyone loved Danny, my fun-loving brother.

As he was growing up, Danny was what people say is an All-American boy. He achieved at just about everything he tried: science fair winner, medal-winning sprinter, top basketball player in high school and college, a debater, and valedictorian of his class. Just before Danny graduated from college, our mother died of cancer. He had the courage to stand up and give her a wonderful eulogy at her funeral. He talked about our mother's sense of humor, and he told the people who came for the service that we should cry and laugh that day. He said that grief and laughter were two sides of the whole, that both gave meaning to our lives. He reminded all of us that it is important to keep a sense of humor even when our hearts are broken. I was so proud of him that day.

Three weeks later Danny delivered the commencement address at his graduation. He put a lot of thought into his speech, emphasizing that it was necessary, as new graduates fresh out in the "real world," to be authentic and real. I especially recall one part — what I call the "three Cs" of his speech: "We may face tough times ahead, but we must remember to meet the challenges with courage, confidence and compassion."

After that, Danny went to graduate school to study international business. He was always interested in global issues. He even took off one semester to travel around Asia in order to learn more about Asian economies. He wrote me saying he was very disturbed by the poverty he saw in the region.

Although a lot of prestigious investment firms in the United States and Europe courted him, Danny's deep loyalty to his family and his love for New York City kept him here. He ended up going to work for a firm that was based at the World Trade Center. Like everything else he did, he was very successful in his work and was quickly promoted to a management position.

Two years ago Danny married Jean, his high school sweetheart. Last week he called me to tell me that on his 30th birthday they were planning to announce the exciting news that they were expecting their first child. That would have been this weekend.

On September 11, Danny went to work early so he could prepare for a big presentation later that day. Some of his colleagues, who got safely out of the North Tower, told me that Danny seemed to be everywhere helping people get out of the building. They remarked how calm he had been, full of his usual confidence and courage as he helped people along. One of his colleagues saw Danny heading back up the stairs and yelled at him, "Hey, where are you going?" Danny's answer: "I just want to be sure everyone got out okay. We need our full team."

Of course, I'm devastated about Danny's death. In fact, I feel like my heart has been broken into lots of little shredded pieces. It is a terrible waste to lose such a gifted man with so much talent and love. But, for some reason, I don't feel enraged or bitter. I guess it's because I believe Danny was a hero, along with all the other innocent people who died in the attack on the Twin Towers. I refuse to think that they died in vain. I am hopeful that their deaths will serve as a wake-up call for all of us to be more thoughtful, to take a hard look at our values, to try to understand who we are — as individuals, as well as citizens of this nation and the world.

Perhaps we need to take time to reflect on what blessings we have taken for granted, what we have done that has been good — and bad — where we are going, where we should go.

I'm sure that Danny would want us to think about what we should do — not to retaliate in rage, but to respond in a way that will make this world a better place for everyone. I keep remembering what he said in his commencement address about facing tough times: "We must try to meet the challenges with courage, confidence and compassion." That's what Danny did when he died helping others in the North Tower. He showed us hope and compassion. Now that's what we must do.

Dark times can catapult us into higher levels of consciousness. We can become stronger, wiser, more compassionate.

– Kathleen Brehony

As I thanked Maureen for sharing the inspiring and healing story of Danny, she looked at me for a moment before she replied. "Thank you for letting me tell my story about my brother. I didn't think I needed to do that, but it has helped me. Maybe we all need to tell or to hear stories. Perhaps if we put a lot of stories of love and hope together, we will heal some of our painful memories of the loss of so many wonderful people in the World Trade Towers."

Yes, Maureen, we will try to do that. And, using your example, we will try to transform our suffering and pain into wisdom, hope and compassion.

GARY

Tower of Courage

I have learned that the way to heal your self is not to focus on your own difficulties but to give your self in service to others.
— Gary

Gary, a former actor, is a tall, handsome New Yorker with a warm smile on his face and a deep interest in people. While on vacation with his family in Ohio during the first week of September 2001, he broke out with painful blisters. The diagnosis: a bad case of shingles (a viral disease characterized by the eruption of small blisters on the skin along the course of a nerve). The doctor said that Gary would likely have them for at least six to eight weeks. Although the doctor offered to prescribe painkillers to make him feel more comfortable, Gary refused to take them. As a recovering alcoholic and drug addict, he wasn't willing to take any chances.

At a party with other AA (Alcoholics Anonymous) members in Ohio, Gary celebrated his three-year anniversary of being clean and sober. He was given a three-year sobriety coin. As his friends enthusiastically congratulated and hugged him, Gary could feel some of the blisters crack open on his back. Even though very painful, he didn't mind the loving bear hugs. He was positive about one thing: Love heals.

On September 10, Gary returned to New York City — a day earlier than scheduled. He wasn't quite sure why he felt compelled to go then, but he knew he needed to return to Manhattan before September 11, the day New York City was attacked by terrorists.

Gary

On September 11, I was feeling tired from my trip, but it was clear in my mind that I was supposed to go to work that day. I got right into my usual routine: the E train subway to the World Trade Center for my traditional oatmeal breakfast at 8:30 at Fine and Shapiro's Deli in the grand concourse of the South Tower. While there I saw and talked with some of my friends who worked in the Towers. Around 8:45, I called my mother in Ohio to tell her I was safely back in the City.

Recently my office was moved out of the South Tower of the World Trade Center to Jersey City. As my mother and I were talking on the phone, she asked: "What's all that commotion? Gary, are you on your way to work? You're supposed to be on vacation one more day. Your shingles are not well enough for you to be going to work. You get back on that train and go home to rest." We laughed, and I went on down the steep escalator into the basement of the South Tower to the PATH train for the ride under the Hudson River to my office.

By the time I got out of the tunnel and arrived at my office a few minutes later, the first tower had been hit. For a few minutes we thought a terrible accident had occurred when the first plane crashed. Being a Wall Street brokerage firm, we had constant access to breaking news, and suddenly word started going around that the U. S. was being attacked. We stood and watched in horror as the second tower was struck. Soon we were shepherded outside, and as we stood there trying to decide how we could get home, the first building collapsed. It seemed impossible that only a few minutes earlier I had been eating my oatmeal there and talking with my friends who were on their way to work in the Towers.

The only thing I could think of doing was to pray the prayer that I say almost every day: "God, I offer myself to Thee — To do with me as Thou wilt. Relieve me of the bondage of self, that I may better do Thy will" (from The Third Step Prayer, *Big Book of Alcoholics Anonymous*). At that point, I decided to begin walking. I figured if God wanted to use me I would walk into an opportunity of service.

By 10:30 I found myself in downtown Hoboken about the same time that one of the triages was being established by Red Cross volunteers, emergency workers, police, and health workers. I was one of the first civilian volunteers to arrive at the site. Although I felt tired and in pain from my shingles, I knew I had to do whatever I could to help. It was interesting that I was told to leave my briefcase and other belongings in the "God Save Our Planet" bar, which was right across the street from the triage. Then I was given a white protective suit and rubber gloves and told to get to work. I was to listen to people, talk with them, help carry food and drinks, and do whatever I was asked.

The survivors from the Towers were being brought across the Hudson River in private boats, ferries, Circle Line boats. Hundreds, maybe thousands, of people had been badly wounded. Most seemed baffled, bewildered and confused about what was happening. Some had been hit by debris falling from the Towers, and they were covered in white ash. The military set up an area where people were sprayed with detoxification materials.

All volunteers at the triage site were given tags to indicate what their function was. My tag had a Purple Cross on it, which meant that my job was to provide some kind of "pastoral care" to the victims. Strangely, I felt qualified to do that because I'd already been through hell myself, and I lived to tell about it. Those people at the World Trade Center had certainly experienced hell that day. I believe it's difficult to be helped by someone who hasn't been there themselves. My experiences in recovery and AA were also useful because I've learned how to listen to others who suffer from fear and confusion.

At one point I saw a man who was totally covered with ash. It seemed strange but he had an oddly joyful grin on his face. When I asked him if he wanted to talk about what had happened, he took out a business card from his pocket and said, "My name is John, and you will be the first person to hear my story."

Shortly after he arrived in his office on the 84th floor of the first Tower to be hit, he heard a deafening crash. His desk was thrown across the room toward the window. As he looked out, he saw the sky was filled with papers, huge fireballs, debris, smoke. "I was the fire marshal for my office, so I grabbed my flashlight, put on my hat and told everyone to form a human chain and follow me. Just about then everything went pitch-black. It was impossible to see even a few inches in front of our faces.

"As we entered the stairwell, someone yelled that we couldn't get through there because a man was pinned under some kind of fallen beam. I don't know where I got the strength to do it, but I was able to get the man free and I picked him up. The next thing I knew some 'eight footers' had picked us up and flew us down the stairs. Before I knew it, all of us were safely down the stairs."

When I asked him what he meant by "eight footers," he answered, "Oh, you know, those great big eight-foot angels. I have no idea how we got down or how I managed to carry that man all the way down those 84 flights of stairs. But suddenly we were on the street outside the building. It felt like a miracle." It felt like a miracle to me too.

Often as I worked through the day, my thoughts went back to the time not many years ago when I had lost my home because of my alcohol and drug abuse. For a while, I was homeless. I felt beaten physically, mentally and spiritually. My heart held no hope. It seemed my life was over when, in fact, it was just beginning. There in the Hoboken Triage I was being used to comfort and give hope to hundreds of people who were feeling hopeless, confused and in great pain — just like I had not long ago. It felt like I was a wounded healer.

Late in the day when I was taking a break, one of the emergency health workers who was dressed in blue hospital clothes sat down beside me. He looked exhausted when he turned to me and said, "Boy, would I like a drink. But I just can't do that." He was a recovering alcoholic, like me. "I'm feeling a little sorry for myself," he confessed. "Tonight I was going to have a big party to celebrate my three years of sobriety, but I won't make it. I need to be here."

Without even thinking about it, I reached into my pocket and took out my recently earned three-year sobriety coin, which I had slipped into my pocket earlier that morning. I took his hand and put the coin in it. "Well, this is your three-year anniversary award. Congratulations, here's your coin. You certainly deserved it," was all I could say. We hugged each other and promised to remember our mutual three-year anniversary "celebration."

After midnight, dazed and exhausted, I finally reached my apartment. It had been a very long and difficult day. My body ached, and I was covered with ashes, dirt and blood. Although I desperately wanted to fall into my bed and into a deep sleep, I knew I needed to take a long hot shower. As I rinsed the soap from my tired body, I was amazed to see that my shingles had turned into scabs. Standing under the warm shower, I watched in wonder as the water washed those scabs off my body and down the drain.

Somehow I had been miraculously healed of the shingles. But that healing seemed small compared to the spiritual healing that took place inside me that day. I began to understand that the more I listened, the more people I hugged, the more people who were helped by my being with them in that triage, the more strength I seemed to get. Most importantly, I learned that the way to heal your self is not to focus on your own difficulties but to give your self in service to others.

Being brave does not mean being unafraid. It often means being afraid and doing it anyway.

– Rachel Naomi Remen

On that dark Tuesday of September 11, 2001, there may have been many people who wanted to flee as fast as possible from the area of the terrible disaster at the World Trade Center. But Gary knew that his purpose that day was to be present, to turn around, to head to where help was needed. He was ready to be of service even though he was experiencing his own pain and illness.

Sometimes, like Gary, when we are tired, exhausted, and hurting from our tribulations and afflictions, we may find that reaching out and helping others in need is the most healing thing we can do for ourselves — and for others. By responding with courage and compassion to suffering and loss, we may find deeper meaning and significance in our lives.

BOBBY

Tower of
Reconciliation

*By returning to Vietnam when it was not a war situation and they were
not the "enemy." I found the people were forgiving, loving, sensitive.
We realized how much we had in common, having experienced
the pain, the agony and the reality of war.*
— Bobby

Long before I ever met Bobby, our paths were destined to cross through
our involvement in a country on the other side of the world: Vietnam.
In the late-1980s, while I was working at Save the Children, the needs
of children in Vietnam were coming to our attention. Vietnam was then
one of the world's five poorest countries, and nearly 40 percent of its
children were malnourished.

But there were major barriers to establishing a program since
Vietnam and the U.S. had no diplomatic relations at the time. And for
many Americans the word "Vietnam" had the power to bring up memories
of deep pain and unhealed scars of a bummer war, MIAs, Agent Orange,
the "enemy."

As I worked to launch Save's new program, I had many experiences in Vietnam that taught me a lot about forgiveness and healing. One person who helped me reframe Vietnam was Bobby, a well-known, positive-spirited, Vietnam veteran in a wheelchair and president of the Vietnam Veterans of America Foundation.

Bobby

In 1964 when I was in my freshman year of college, most Americans supported the Vietnam War. People don't generally remember that because later the war went so sour. There was an almost bizarre mentality that was somewhat captured by President Kennedy: "Pay any price, bear any burden, to advance freedom around the world." When I was a senior, my business professor told our class that combat experience in the service would be a tremendous asset to a management career in corporate America.

Being physically fit, mentally sound and a graduate of college, I knew I would inevitably be drafted. One day I walked into the student union, and there was a Marine Corps recruiter wearing his snazzy, dress blue uniform. The guy looked like he was over 6 feet tall and at least 200 pounds. So I fell for the propaganda that the Marines were elite and special.

In training we were told that 85 percent of Marine junior officers in Vietnam were being realized as casualties. In the squad bay at night we didn't debate whether or not we would be casualties. We debated how we would handle being blind, losing a leg or being powerless. I remember saying with conviction that if I lost a leg I wanted someone to kill me. Now I look at an amputee as light stuff, not even a minor inconvenience.

It's amazing what can happen out on a parade deck with a bunch of guys doing drills, fixing bayonets and yelling out exercises like: "What's the point of a bayonet?" "To kill." "Who do you kill?" "Luke the Gook." "Who?" "Link the Chink." There's something frightfully powerful and exciting about learning how to throw hand grenades, fire machine guns or rifles, or fire off a few high-caliber weapons. Meanwhile, you're being told stories about guys who graduated ahead of you who were mutilated by the VC (Viet Cong) or who were coming back from Vietnam in body bags.

During my tour of duty in Vietnam there were a number of incidents that caused me to realize that I had gone through some real head changes and had taken a journey down a dark path. One evening my unit set up an operation around a village. Some kids came by, and we gave them candy bars and other things. That night we were attacked by someone who clearly knew our operations. The kids must have informed the VC where our positions were and what our strength was. The payback for opening up to the kids wasn't good.

Later when my men were on trucks moving in a convoy, some guys took out the heating tablets we used to warm our C rations, the food we carried. When lit, the tablets burned like the stuff in a barbecue pit, but you couldn't see the flame. Several guys lit these tabs and threw them off the truck. The Vietnamese kids picked them up and were burned as the tabs stuck to their hands. I remember laughing when I saw that happen. That seemed strange to me because I had always been very sensitive and loving to children.

Looking back, I realize that I had become warped and capable of doing weird things — even though I had once been a little leaguer, a "good guy." Having experienced that dark path and how it changed who I was gave me some insight about the "good guy" soldiers who went into My Lai and undertook a massacre, murdering 500 people without a single shot being returned. It's possible for me to comprehend that we are capable of both extraordinary altruistic actions and terrible evil.

At that point, I was no longer fighting for reasons of patriotism or politics. I was fighting because the enemy was wearing a different color uniform than we did. The dividing line between good guys and bad guys was determined by their uniforms. Whether the war was right or wrong didn't alter it for me. I just got up in the morning, went out on patrol, jumped on a helicopter and flew to another landing zone.

Although the idea of quitting hadn't crossed my mind as an option, the war was starting to unravel for me. My experiences brought home that it just didn't make sense. Whenever we got into a firefight with North Vietnamese troops, the South Vietnamese battalions often broke contact and ran. Other times the SV officers went up and down the line of their troops kicking and whipping them with sticks to get them to move. The people in the villages certainly didn't support us or want us there. The whole thing was screwy. But it was not until I was totally extracted from that environment that I could reflect on it and ask questions that I'd never asked on the front end.

The day I got shot was April 29, 1969. I had been in Vietnam since the beginning of September, 1968. We were on a combined operation with 500-plus South Vietnamese soldiers who were working with U.S. Marines. There were ten Marine tanks, eight gun tanks and two flame tanks. We were moving through an area right below the demilitarized zone. There was a "suicide squad" of North Vietnamese soldiers left on a hill to block our advance. They were hard-core guys who had dug in while the rest of their unit was leaving the area. As usual, trying to get the South Vietnamese battalions to assault turned out to be almost impossible.

Earlier that afternoon a guy had come up to me and said, "Are you Lieutenant Muller? They've been looking for you for weeks. They want you back at Marine Corps headquarters, and I'm your replacement. You can get out of here." And I told him, "Hold on. I'm in the middle of something and have to finish it."

As standard fare I called in some artillery, and for an hour and a half there was heavy shooting right on that hilltop. Jets dropped big bombs, the gun tanks used a lot of their ammunition, and a flame tank burned the hill. We literally pounded the daylights out of those soldiers. The tank commanders reported that during the afternoon they saw those guys pop up now and then and many were bleeding from their heads. A lot of stuff was dumped on them, but we didn't kill them. When people really dug into a hole, they could take a lot of pounding. If you tried the easy way of dropping bombs on them, you usually pissed them off. It was not a solution.

Although we had a lot of guys who were already shot and messed up, I had a colonel on my case who kept saying, "Take the hill. Take the hill." So I told our tank commanders to lay down a base of fire because the only way we could get those guys who had dug in was to dig them out. We had to walk up the hill and do the job. I remember thinking, "You know what? I'm going to get you."

So we started to move out. But as I headed up that hill, I took a bullet through my chest. It went through both lungs and severed my spinal cord on the way out the other side. I didn't know what had happened. It wasn't painful; it felt like I was in some kind of kaleidoscope. Everything was multi-colored and fragmented, like the windshield of a car shattered into a thousand pieces all jumbled together. I was lying on the ground and looking up at the sky. I remember grabbing my abdomen, not feeling anything, and thinking "I must have taken it through my gut."

All of a sudden I felt super-duper calm and unbelievably relaxed — a warm glowing sensation. Plus I had the feeling that I was deflating. In fact I was, because both of my lungs were collapsing. I felt myself going down. I realized that I was going to die, and there was absolutely nothing I could do to stop what felt like a slide down a chute. "I'm going down, I'm leaving, I'm out of here." There was nothing I could grab onto, there was nothing I could take with me, it was just me by myself. I was absolutely 1,000 percent sure that I was dying. My last conscious thought: "I can't believe it. I'm going to die on this shitty piece of ground."

It turned out there was an Australian who was part of my unit who dragged me down from the hill. I had already ordered medical evacuation helicopters that were enroute, so I was medivaced minutes after being shot. It was my good luck that the Third Medical Battalion was very close by. From there I was immediately sent to the hospital ship USS Repose, which that afternoon was as far north as it ever went and was just turning to go back south to Danang. Later I learned from my medical records that if I had arrived one minute later I would have died because both lungs had collapsed. That injury, more than my severed spinal cord, was life-threatening.

When I woke up on the hospital ship, I couldn't believe I was awake. I almost didn't believe I was alive. I was as close to euphoria as I could imagine.

Several days later a doctor told me, "I've got good news and bad news. The good news is that we're quite confident you're going to live." To that I laughed: "I could have told you that as soon as I woke up!" Obviously the jury had been out on that for several days. Then he added, "But in all likelihood, you're going to be paralyzed." I immediately responded, "That's okay. I can handle that." Being paralyzed wasn't the issue. The issue was that I was alive. I already knew I was paralyzed by the time I talked with that doctor, because I was in a striper frame and was being rotated every few hours.

The care I got on the hospital ship was extraordinary. In the Intensive Care Unit, there was always someone there. After the hospital ship, I was flown to St. Alban's Hospital. A lot of active-duty people who worked there had either been in Vietnam or were on their way. They were very sensitive and took good care of me. The hospital had discipline and structure, and it was a caring place.

One day I was put into an ambulance and driven from St. Alban's in the Queens to a veterans' hospital. There were enormous differences between the military and the veterans' hospitals. The positive stuff about the military hospital — the discipline, the respect I had as a lieutenant, the corpsmen's sensitivity — were gone. I went from being somebody in the military hospital to being nobody in the veterans' hospital. I was no longer Lieutenant Muller. I was just a veteran. That was the first day I cried.

The hospital itself was hardly conducive to healing. It was a dilapidated old building, it smelled, it was dark and overcrowded, and it was depressing. There weren't many soldiers or young guys; there were a lot of old men and other patients who had no other medical provider for their care. They were the down and outs: alcoholics, automobile accident victims, crazy people.

My first night there, the guy in the next bed ranted and raved at the ceiling and made all kinds of noises. When I told the nurse, "This guy is out of his mind," I was told he was a paraplegic because he had jumped off the roof of a mental institution and broken his back. Another roommate had been involved with a robbery and had a knife stuck in his back.

Just days before I left the military hospital, I had been put in a wheelchair for the first time. Usually they are symbols of terrible things, but when you've been in a bed for a long time and finally can go down the hallway in a wheelchair to a soda machine, it's the greatest liberation in the world.

After I was transferred to the Veterans' Hospital and had been in bed for several hours, I wanted to get up. The afternoon shift had just changed, and the new guy said, "We don't have a wheelchair for you. And I'm busy." I was on a ward with thirty spinal injury patients all needing wheelchairs. When he told me they didn't have a wheelchair, I told him to find one. I yelled and swore at him, and he told me not to raise my voice. Of course, it escalated.

Finally, with enough screaming, he got me a wheelchair. But I couldn't yet get in and out of a wheelchair without help, and he didn't want to take ten seconds to hold my feet while I slid my rear end into the chair, which led to another confrontation. That was my first day. When my mother came later to visit me, she wept hysterically. She couldn't believe that I was in such a depressing place.

The next day was grand rounds with the chief doctor for physical medicine and rehabilitation services. Someone handed him a three-by-five card that he looked at briefly before saying, "Lieutenant Muller. Well, son, I hope you realize that you are hopelessly paralyzed." I just looked at him with my mouth open.

In the military hospital I had neurosurgeons who had explained in detail that because I was so critically wounded they had never opened up the spinal cord area at the injury point and performed a laminectomy. Therefore they were unable to determine what damage had been done to the spinal cord, but there might be some return of function. They would only know that with the passage of time. After the chief doctor came out with his statement about my being hopelessly paralyzed, everybody walked away. I was left speechless.

In the mornings I did physical therapy with two good therapists. But we had only one set of parallel bars, one mat area, one wall unit, and fifteen patients trying to use them with only two therapists. I ended up sitting around a lot and waiting for one of them to work with me. I worked my ass off — I really tried. I wanted braces because I wanted to try to ambulate with crutches. The chief doctor told me I shouldn't bother to try; it would be a waste of time.

A visiting doctor, who had caught a piece of shrapnel in his back during the Second World War, came to a consultation. He was a paraplegic and wore braces underneath his pants. He had some limited mobility. He asked me how I was doing. I told him "lousy," that I wanted to try to do some ambulation but the chief doctor wouldn't authorize braces for me. The visiting doctor lambasted the chief doctor, saying, "Whenever somebody wants to try, it's not for you to tell them they can't do it. This guy deserves the right to try." Eventually I got braces and did a lot of good therapy with them.

Although I didn't have to stay that long, I remained in the hospital one year for rehabilitative purposes. I wanted to try everything to put my life back together as best I could and to "walk" out of there. I gave the braces my best shot. Finally I admitted, "The braces aren't working. It's not worth the effort, the time, the energy, and I want to move on." But I left with a peace of mind that I had made the right decision.

In May 1970, *Life Magazine* did a centerpiece story about my hospital ward. Because I was college educated and could speak well, I was selected to be the spokesman. It was the second largest-selling issue the magazine had ever turned out. After the story appeared in *Life*, I ended up doing a lot of media work because I had the "right stuff" — a Marine Infantry officer who had been shot assaulting the enemy. The piece triggered a public outrage that was followed by congressional hearings and a lot of media opportunities.

Because I was advocating for the plight of veterans in hospitals, other vets from the movement started contacting me. The more we talked, the more I realized that what I had gone through wasn't unique. My feelings seemed similar to theirs. Soon I became a representative of how the whole thing was screwed up, and I began speaking out against the war.

Although hundreds of guys came together for anti-war marches or demonstrations, the media always selected the guys in wheechairs or those who were visibly disabled to put at the head of the parades. The reporters wanted someone to provide the visuals along with the rap, and I was made-to-order and my obvious disability gave me credibility to speak. Before long I became a speaker for the Vietnam Veterans against the War (VVAW).

Many guys didn't want to talk against the war because they thought it wouldn't show respect for the guys who had died; it was like saying their deaths had been for nothing. Initially people thought that I was speaking because I was angry about being a paraplegic. I explained that it was very difficult for me to speak out against the war because I was admitting that the price I had paid was for nothing. It would have been easier to wrap myself in the mantle of being a disabled hero.

The public mainly saw the VVAW as veterans who opposed the war. While that was a common denominator, the VVAW also provided us an important opportunity to get together and talk about our experiences. It was like a continuous rap session to express our anger and work through a lot of pain. It was tremendously therapeutic to end the isolation and to learn, "I'm not the only one who had a bummer of a trip. It was a shared experience."

Eventually the rap groups were recognized as a pioneering effort, a new form of counseling that we had come across naturally. They gave rise to vets' centers, a fairly innovative approach dealing with post traumatic stress disorder (PTSD). Talking and working through the feelings again and again with others who understood where you were coming from helped people get it out of their system.

A national survey conducted in the 1970s and 1980s revealed that the overwhelming majority of Vietnam veterans never talked about their war experience once they returned home. Because I spent years with other vets in continuous rap groups, I couldn't imagine what it was like for the vets who still had those emotions bottled up inside and didn't have the chance for such a cathartic aspect.

When I went to Washington in 1978, I started the Vietnam Veterans of America (VVA) — the only congressionally chartered national organization for Vietnam vets.

On Memorial Day in 1979, I gave a speech on the steps of City Hall in New York. "You people ran a number on us," I told the assembled crowd. "Your guilt, your hang-ups, your uneasiness have made it socially unacceptable for us to mention that we were Vietnam veterans. Whenever we bring it up, you walk away from the conversation." That struck a chord that resonated with a lot of people, and the story wound up on the front page of the *New York Times*. Certainly the war was a negative experience, something people wanted to avoid. But there were a lot of people who couldn't walk away from it.

The movement for Vietnam vets began to turn around when the hostages came back from Iran and were given a New York City ticker tape parade. I was in our New York office that day, and the phones were ringing off the hook. People were upset at what was being done for the returning hostages as compared to what had not been done for the Vietnam vets, and they wanted to balance the scales. The same kind of public outrage reached the Congress. Members of the Committee on Veterans' Affairs said that for the first time they received bags of mail urging them to do something for Vietnam veterans. At last it was okay to talk about the Vietnam War, which eventually brought sympathy and support for the vets.

There are many vets like me: all-American obedient and trusting kids who tried to do the right thing. We thought the U.S. was a great country, about freedom, democracy and civil rights. When the government said, "We've got to help some freedom-loving people in South Vietnam," what did we know? We just did it.

For me, being disabled was not an issue. What I needed healing from was having been a part of a war that was a lie. I went to Vietnam in good faith, only to realize later my faith had been abused. It's been documented that the government did not tell the truth about what was going on. They knew long before I ever joined the service that Vietnam was a lost war. But still we continued to fight, and a million people died.

Why was I able to heal from that lie while others had more difficulty? For one thing, I didn't come back and pretend that stuff hadn't happened. I didn't bury it deep inside so it could continue to rattle around and percolate to the surface ten or fifteen years later. The phenomenon of post-traumatic stress can easily take that long. Certainly my healing process was advanced by the opportunity to work through my emotions with others who had gone through similar experiences in Vietnam. Then the feelings started to lose their force and weren't as gripping as they had been when they were a rage. Connecting with other guys helped me understand that my bad experience was shared. And the years of public speaking — sometimes as many as three times a day to high schools, civic groups, and religious organizations — were cathartic and healing. Finally, I did some reading and research about what had really happened in Vietnam. Everything helped.

Although I had been a forceful anti-war spokesperson, was thrown out of the Republican Convention in 1972, and did lots of radical stuff, to tell the truth, I had a personal resentment and bitterness about the Vietnamese. I thought everything about them was rotten. Even though I knew the U.S. was wrong to have been there, I just didn't like the people. Certainly in our training the Vietnamese had been completely dehumanized, and during the war the people had not received us as heroes, liberators and protectors as I, in my naive way, had hoped. Of course, we really weren't, because we were the ones who were smashing them.

Also, my exposure in Vietnam was rather "skewed." I had been in a very hostile area at the height of the war in 1968-69. As advisors to the South Vietnamese Army working with its commanding officers, we had to have personal bodyguards around us all night because we knew a good 15 percent of the troops were Viet Cong. In the morning, guys would be missing who had taken as many supplies as they could carry. So we never knew who was a "bad guy."

In 1981, when I led the first group of American veterans back to Vietnam, I went through one of the most profound experiences of my life. This time I was able to meet and talk with the people. In a space of less than two days, they went from being people I didn't like at all to people I really liked. By returning when it was not a war situation and they were not "the enemy," I found the people were forgiving, loving, sensitive and wonderful. It took no time at all to see that.

On our last night in Hanoi, we had a discussion with a group of Vietnamese veterans about the MIA problem, a political issue in the

States. There were four of us on one side of the table and six of them on the other. I told them we needed to return to the States with some bones of Americans, or the trip would not be viewed as successful. This triggered a discussion about MIAs. They began to tell us their stories, about their problems, about their brothers, and what it meant to have them missing. There are over 300,000 Vietnamese MIAs.

Those six guys opened up their shirts, and we saw bullet or shrapnel wounds on each one of them. We realized how much we had in common, having experienced the pain, the agony and the reality of the war. We knew what they were talking about; we had been there. That common bond was more important than the political differences between us. It was an unbelievable catharsis to look those guys in the eye and understand what we shared. We ended up bursting into tears and hugging each other. It was a powerful and healing moment.

As a result of that trip, we helped hundreds of other vets go back to Vietnam. Every one has benefited by returning. In almost every case, there have been aspects of healing through reconciliation with the former enemy, by replacing and updating time-frozen images with a reality that was not negative, and through the opportunity to deal with and ultimately let go of bad stuff. Certainly I would urge every vet to go back to Vietnam, if possible, because connecting to a country during a war is a limited connect. The beauty and the grace of the people and the land continue to be powerful healing aspects.

For me, letting go of the animosity was like getting rid of a weight around my neck. By letting go of bitterness, remorse and negative stuff, I was lightened up and healed. If I had continued to cling to the past and its pain, I would have drained myself and blocked my healing. But in order to let it go, I had to confront my pain and deal with it. The idea that someone can deny something because "it's no big thing" doesn't work because it's still undermining things. I'm not saying someone should forget, but I am saying forgive. To go through forgiveness and to have reconciliation are very positive experiences.

Many people who have suffered tremendous difficulties in their lives view those experiences in terms of loss. But I view my experience in terms of what I got back: my life. When I was at the Veterans' Hospital I briefly went to a psychologist. The psychologist thought I was crazy since I wasn't despondent, that I was denying the loss of the use of half my body, that I was overly compensating by working out in rehabilitation programs. I kept telling her, "You look at me in terms of the glass being half empty. I look at myself in terms of what I have! My life!"

I think back to my days in training and how I said, "If I ever lose a leg, I want someone to kill me." Ha! I didn't want to die! When we get up in the morning, we deny the truth that we are all going to die. On some level we recognize that life is finite and we will die, but we honestly don't live life being connected to that reality. I believe we would benefit by doing that.

On that hill in Vietnam I truly accepted my mortality and thought I had cashed out. Because things miraculously came together, I was given a second chance. So it's all borrowed time, it's all a bonus, and I'm grateful. How many people died in that war with far less injuries than I had?

We have only so much time and so much energy in life. We can squander it by fighting back and being negative, or we can use it to build and go forward. I'm putting my faith in the basic goodness of life.

Healing is embracing what is most feared. Healing is opening what has been closed.

— Jeanne Achterberg

As the all-American good guy who had wanted to do the right thing, Bobby found the physical shattering of his body easier to cope with than the crushing of his patriotic convictions when he realized the political myth about the war was not true. He had a lot of work to do to heal the massive scars of physical, emotional and political injuries. By publicly telling his story and meeting with Vietnamese veterans — whom he thought were his enemies — he found peace and reconciliation in what he learned was authentic and genuine.

A healing process from such extensive pain usually begins when we choose to face the truth and stop pretending that bad things haven't happened. Like Bobby, we can let go of our delusions and fantasies by educating ourselves with the truth. This may help us fight off negativity and pessimism. We too can discover how to live with our limitations, accept our mortality and still be grateful for the gift of life.

Today Bobby dedicates himself to assisting those who were injured by the war — including his former enemies. His work as co-founder of the International Campaign to Ban Landmines has resulted in the signing of a comprehensive landmine ban treaty and the awarding of the Nobel Peace Prize to the organization in 1997.

Noreen

Tower of Forgiveness

Bitterness is one of the dreadful burdens that many people have when something bad happens — especially if they aren't able to forgive. Although I may have asked why this terrible thing happened, I've never felt that the bomb was God's doing.
— Noreen

More than 25 years ago while attending an international conference in Dar es Salaam, Tanzania, I met Dermod McCarthy, an Irish filmmaker and priest. We first connected during a lesson in Swahili under an ancient Banyan tree. We became conference buddies and later lifelong friends. Over the years, Dermod described the anguish and frustration that the people of Ireland have experienced from nearly 30 years of conflict and violence. He shared stories of tragic losses of life, of visits to hospitals and prisons on both sides of the border, and of countless efforts to reach a permanent peace in Northern Ireland.

Dermod also told me many inspiring and heroic stories filled with compassion, faith and forgiveness. One that especially stood out was about

Noreen, a courageous woman whose husband Ronnie had been in a coma since 1987 when an IRA bomb exploded in Enniskillen. He was standing with a crowd of people at an annual Remembrance Ceremony. A colossal bomb planted inside the nearby community centre blew apart a heavy brick wall that fell onto the crowd, pinning many under piles of debris. The explosion killed eleven people and injured sixty-three others. After thirteen years in a coma, Ronnie died peacefully on December 28, 2000.

When I heard parts of Noreen's story, I knew I wanted to include it in this book of healing. So I traveled to Northern Ireland to interview her.

Noreen

I'm always introduced as Noreen Hill, wife of Ronnie Hill, the headmaster of the Enniskillen High School who was seriously injured in the Enniskillen bombing of November 8, 1987.

I was born in Northern Ireland, and Ronnie was born in Dublin in the South. We moved around a lot because of his work as a teacher, vice principal, and then a headmaster. Ronnie was very good at his work. Although there were a lot of naughty children in the schools, Ronnie always said, "There is no bad child. There is no child who doesn't have something." He looked to find the good in someone and to bring that out. People remember him as a very conscientious headmaster. Years before the peace agreement, he was working with both the Catholic and Protestant schools, bringing them together, because he knew that would help the peace process. An officer of the Western Area Education Board said, "Ronnie was ahead of his time. He could see what should be happening."

Ronnie and I moved to Enniskillen in 1974 because he was made the headmaster of the high school. We lived there until the time of the IRA bombing on November 8, 1987.

In February of that year I had surgery for a fast-growing breast cancer. By September I had just completed my chemo and radiotherapy treatments. I had been really ill with the chemotherapy so I was very weak.

On Sunday, November 8, my aunt and sister were coming to our house to help take care of me, so I didn't go with Ronnie to the Memorial Service. As usual, he left the house about 9:50 and went to our Presbyterian Church. Later he went to the Cenotaph (a memorial erected in remembrance of people whose graves are located elsewhere), which was a couple hundred yards from our church, to attend the War Memorial Service in honor of the men who died in the First and Second World Wars. Both Catholics and Protestants were remembered.

I was at home waiting for my aunt when I heard the bomb. I knew it was at the service, and in my heart I knew that Ronnie was injured. Perhaps I was in shock or maybe God was protecting me, but I didn't feel any fear. Certainly I was being looked after, because my aunt and sister were already on their way to stay with us.

At the hospital I found Ronnie in x-ray. A wall had fallen on him and many other people. He was completely buried except for a gloved hand. When they started digging out those who were buried, they saw his hand and they dug him out. He needed surgery; the bridge of his nose was broken; he had 37 stitches around his head; he had a fractured jaw, a fractured shoulder, a fractured skull and a fractured pelvis. He also suffered from bomb blast trauma. He was not yet unconscious, but he couldn't really speak because of the fractured jaw.

When I first was told in the hospital that Ronnie would not see the morning, I prayed a lot. I felt numb. You know how the brain protects itself during terrible happenings.

Ronnie was airlifted to Altnagelvin Hospital in Londonderry where he stayed for five weeks. The Tuesday after the bombing he went into a coma. That night he was put on a life-support machine and was off and on it for nearly five weeks. During that time I stayed in the hospital with him day and night. I only went home on weekends and spent one night there before returning to the hospital. I was thankful my aunt and sister were staying with my daughter.

Every Thursday Ronnie seemed to take a dip in the evening and we were told that he probably wouldn't see morning, but every Friday morning he was still with us. On Thursday of the fifth week, Ronnie was doing great and didn't need to be on the life-support machine. The next morning he was moved to the Erne Hospital in Enniskillen where he stayed for four and a half years. During those years, I spent most of my time in the hospital.

In the hospital, I read to Ronnie, talked to him and played his favorite music on a tape recorder. Many people from all over the world sent us tapes, including healing tapes, that we played. When I left Ronnie at night, I'd say my prayers, leave him with the Lord and go home to sleep.

When Ronnie was able to leave the hospital after four and a half years, we wanted him to be at home where we thought we would have a more "normal life." Because he needed special care around the clock, we decided to buy a residential home that was already set up with beds and nursing care. We knew our family couldn't afford to pay for the costs of two staff 24 hours a day 365 days a year to take care of Ronnie. Also there was less stress for him in a home than in a hospital. My apartment was on the top floor. So whenever anything happened to him, the staff just buzzed me and I was right there. It worked out well for us.

During the day, I was able to see Ronnie anytime, whether it was the first thing in the morning or late at night. Every time I passed his room I stopped in. Sometimes a dozen times in one day. I read to him, prayed with him and made sure he had his favorite music. Occasionally I turned on television programs that I thought might interest him. I knew he listened because he made little noises from time to time.

Although Ronnie was in a coma, he could hear and his senses were acute. At the beginning when people told him things, he started yawning and swallowing. I was embarrassed because I thought he wasn't interested in what they were saying. But it was the only way he could communicate. When he was listening, he yawned. He also opened and closed his eyes and looked around, but he didn't do it to command or respond. Toward the end, his concentration didn't last long, and he went back to sleep very quickly.

Before the bomb, Ronnie had a triple heart bypass and he recovered. Somehow we learned to accept that situation and live with it. After the bomb, we were told many times that Ronnie would be dead before morning, but he was still with us thirteen years later. When he was diagnosed as having heart failure in the twelfth year and given two months to a year to live — sooner than later— it was a shock. It shouldn't have been, because he could have died at any time before then. But in the end we were given the strength we needed.

Sometimes when I looked at Ronnie, I couldn't help but feel sad thinking of what he could have done. After the bombing we prayed for a miracle, and we thought we would get it — that Ronnie would be made whole again. But that didn't happen. If Ronnie had recovered, his story would have been wonderful: all that he went through, how he got through it, how he was restored.

Nobody knows why the IRA chose the Memorial Service as a place to put a bomb. It was a strange place, because the service was honoring both Catholics and Protestants who died in the World Wars. Perhaps there were more Protestants than Catholics at the service, but you wouldn't know that for sure, and you wouldn't have asked. Later we learned the bomb was not supposed to have hit innocent civilians; it was targeted at the British security forces. But where the bomb was planted was too far away to hit any security forces, and it exploded where civilians always stood.

Some people say they're sorry I have to suffer. But suffering has been taken away from me. I believe that can happen to anyone, but you have to be willing to hand it over to God. A lot of people ask God to take away their pain, but then they turn around and take it back themselves again. When you're worried about something, there's no point in asking God to help sort it out and then turn around and worry about it again. Because you've just taken it back again. I think this is why some people feel God leaves them. But God never leaves you. It's you that leaves God. Sometimes in my prayers I'll say, "Lord, I can't feel your presence. But I know it's my fault because I'm just closing my mind to you."

Gordon Wilson's daughter Marie was killed by the Enniskillen bombing, and Gordon himself was injured as he stood beside her. The next morning Gordon came on television and said he forgave the people who did the bombing. A lot of people criticized him for that. Some people said, "Who does Gordon Wilson think he is? Does he think he's God that he can forgive them?" Well, those people may know the Lord's

Prayer, but they also need to read the two verses right after that prayer in the sixth chapter of Matthew. There it says that if you forgive, then the Lord will forgive you. But if you don't forgive, he can't forgive you.

Gordon also said, "I'm at the end of my life, so why did God take Marie and leave me?" But I think Marie wouldn't have been able to come on the media the next morning and make the statement that Gordon did. His statement saved a lot of people. The Enniskillen bombing was such a dreadful atrocity that people who were UDA Loyalists (Ultster Defence Association, the major Protestant paramilitary group, now outlawed) were ready to go out and kill. But when Gordon said what he did, they couldn't do it. I believe that's why he was left and Marie was taken. Gordon had a job to do. We all do!

Ronnie too had an important job. He knew that peace had to start with the children, that our hope for the future is with them. He was instrumental in getting students in different Catholic and Protestant schools to come together, because he wanted kids from both sides to see each other as normal. The schools are still working together today. I hope the seeds he sowed will bear fruit.

When people ask how I can forgive what has happened to our family, I tell them I know my hatred and bitterness have been taken away from me. When I was at the hospital after the bombing, a Catholic woman came up to me and said, "Mrs. Hill, you must have a lot of hatred and anger toward the Catholics." I told her, "I know that our Catholic friends would have laid down their lives to prevent this from happening to Ronnie. There's not one of them who would have wished this on him. So why would I have hatred toward Catholics?" One of the first people I remember seeing at the hospital was the priest Monsignor Cahill. When I looked at him, I didn't see a priest; I didn't see a Catholic. I saw a friend.

Occasionally I have asked God why this terrible thing happened to Ronnie because he was such a fine person. But I never blamed God, nor did I feel that the bomb was God's doing. I also know that bitterness is one of the dreadful burdens that many people have when something bad happens to them — especially if they aren't able to forgive. I believe those burdens should always be handed over to God.

The people who did the bombing have never been caught. I've heard that it's known who they are and where they live. Certainly they need forgiveness. I know I must forgive what they did to us. When someone is murdered, in any country, and the family of the victim can't forgive, that burden is very heavy to bear. Hatred is a barrier to healing.

From time to time I pray for the people who did the bombing in Enniskillen, and I believe I have forgiven them. I've been told here in Northern Ireland when families who have lost loved ones couldn't forgive the people who did it, the people who've been put in prison and weren't ever forgiven were as hard as nails. Nobody could get through to them. But the ones who were forgiven were very different. So no matter what the situation is, we have to forgive.

After a terrible trauma or tragedy people usually come 'round right then or shortly afterwards. It's three months down the road when people are alone at home with no one there — those are the lonely times when they need someone. By that time everybody has picked up and gone on with their own lives. But that's the time the family really needs somebody or something.

I've learned a lot from this experience. I think one of the greatest lessons has been that I should take one day at a time. And yet, I know there will be times when something will happen that might cause anxiety, things that will be difficult and on my mind. But if I go one day at a time, I know I can make it. That's true for everyone. We should all live fully in this day, try not to worry, and give our worries to God.

I have a lovely story I like to tell. Not long ago I was asked to speak at a gathering of people from all over Northern Ireland. There were several speakers, but I was the first to speak. After I finished, the next speaker was an innocent civilian who had both his legs blown off by a bomb that was placed under his car. When he started to speak, I thought, "I've suffered nothing compared to that man. Just look at him." I felt such sympathy for him, because I thought he had suffered so much.

Then he started to speak: "My story is nothing compared to Noreen Hill's. How can I follow after her?" I think maybe that's the answer. If you look at other people and see what they had to do, you will find they always have suffered more than you. At least that's the way I look at it. And I believe that's the way this man looked at it too. He saw that I was left with Ronnie, who was in a coma and could do nothing. Because he could get about in his wheelchair and could go for rides in his car in the country, his suffering seemed nothing to him. So when I hear about other people and what is going on in their lives, I don't think of what's happening to our family as suffering.

If anyone asks my advice on how to cope in painful, sad, or difficult situations, I tell them, don't just think about yourself. It doesn't help to keep saying, "Oh, poor me, poor me. Why did this happen to me?" Well, who are you? Nobody really! The burden of bitterness and hatred is terrible to bear. So just turn everything over to God and forgive. Then carry on from there and take one day at a time after that. Before you know it you'll be back on track again.

———————————————

Violence is not inevitable. Nonviolence, the spirit of love and compassion, lives in the hearts of everyone.

– Mairead Corrigan Maguire

Just before my departure to Northern Ireland, I heard a speech by Nobel Peace Prizewinner Mairead Corrigan Maguire of Belfast, who tirelessly inspired thousands of people to demonstrate against the mindless carnage in Northern Ireland. Her encouraging words about nonviolence and compassion were still echoing in my mind when I interviewed Noreen in her cozy, plant-filled apartment.

At the heart of Noreen's healing story are two key elements. First is her very strong and positive approach to forgiveness and faith. Secondly, she does not entertain thoughts of self-pity or bitterness; she understands that suffering is part of life and that others are in even worse situations than she is.

We can learn a great deal about adversity and healing from Noreen. She asks us a poignant question: "Do we want to heal, or do we want to suffer?" Rather than hang on to suffering, resentments, conflicts and prejudices that harm us, we would do better to forgive our enemies and turn over our hostilities to a higher power. Perhaps we too could free ourselves from the debilitating poisons of wrath, hostility and fear, and we might learn to live in peace. Forgiveness and faith serve as potent antioxidants that have the power to protect us from experiencing the anguish of despair and malice.

Noreen's story is a persuasive tribute to the healing power of faith and forgiveness. It is a beautiful illustration of Mairead Corrigan Maguire's point that violence is not inevitable, that compassion can live in people's hearts.

TULLEY SPOTTED EAGLE BOY
Tower of Vision

I was drinking at the age of nine and was an alcoholic by age fourteen.
When I left Red Bank, I was the Reserve drunk. I was a nobody.
That was how people knew me. But I had a second chance in life.
— Tulley

Without much warning Tulley Spotted Eagle Boy soared into my life — almost like his legendary namesake, the spotted eagle. I first saw this tall Mi'Kmaq medicine man as he walked down the aisle of the Cathedral of St. John the Divine in New York City during the Blessing of the Animals Ceremony on St. Francis Day. When he passed my row, I saw his sculpted face up close for only a few seconds; I sensed that he was a person who had suffered greatly and survived.

I saw him again a few months later in a smoky sweat lodge in upstate New York. I had heard that people could find healing, balance and restoration in a sweat-lodge ceremony. But my initial reaction to the ceremony was that I wouldn't survive! I had never felt such blistering heat in such a cramped space in my entire life. With Tulley leading the ceremony for eight people, I willed myself to "let go" and sweat it out. As he chanted the rhythmic, ancient words calling on the Great Spirit and the spirits of ancestors and animals, I found my fear dissipating and my body relaxing as the sweat poured from every pore of my body. At the end of the ceremony, I felt a sense of tranquility and a deep connection with the universe.

Later that night as I drove back to New York City, I decided I would try to learn more about Tulley Spotted Eagle Boy and the roads he had traveled to find healing. Eventually, I followed the spirit of the spotted eagle and visited Tulley at the Red Bank First Nation Reserve in New Brunswick, Canada.

Tulley

As a child I grew up in a place where there were forests, animals and fish. And there were many spirits. I felt a part of the earth and in touch with animals and nature. I was one with them. I was so blessed.

One day when I was about four or five, an Indian agent came to our home on the reserve and took my three brothers, three sisters and me away from our parents. We were put on a big machine. I didn't even know what it was. I was told it was a train. To me it looked enormous — like a huge iron monster. As the train left the station, we looked out the window at our mother, who was standing there with her hands on her eyes and crying.

We were taken to a residential school where they cut our hair so short that we were almost bald. They scrubbed us hard with wire brushes. At that time I only knew my language of Mi'Kmaq, which was taught at home as part of our culture. Although we were not yet English speaking, whenever we spoke our language, a bar of soap was stuck in our mouths. At the school, we were denied our own culture and language, and sisters and brothers were separated from each other. We weren't allowed to receive anything from the outside world, and we only saw our parents once a year. For years we went through this misery and pain.

By the time I was nine, I was already drinking anything I could get my hands on to escape my sorrow. In 1967 when I was fourteen, I left the school and went back home as an alcoholic. I drank every day of my life. I just couldn't deal with what had happened to me. The school took my culture, my identity, my pride and my spirit from me. All I had left was guilt and shame.

Many native people couldn't live with the guilt they felt. Others went home to find that their parents had become alcoholics. They thought they had done something wrong because their children had been taken away from them. Some of them had gone to the same schools when they were young, and they worried a lot about what was happening to their children. But there was nothing they could do to get them out. They just hoped their children would make it through. There was much shame and guilt.

There are videos and books that document the crimes of the residential schools. Recently the government and churches in Canada have spoken up about the treatment that native people received during their stay at the residential schools. Grants of money have been made to First Nation reserves as reparation for the wrongdoing.

One day when I was sixteen, I was playing with some of my friends in an old sandpit. Suddenly the sand came crashing all over me, and I was literally buried alive. As the sand closed over me, I started to see a long tunnel ahead of me. It felt like I was being pulled through the tunnel toward a bright light. It was so bright that I had to close my eyes. When I opened them, I saw some of my ancestors smiling at me. I wanted to stay there with them, but they told me I had to go back to the earth again. I felt really sad as I went back through the tunnel. Then I woke up and saw my friends staring at me. They looked very frightened as they dug me out of the sandpit.

Even after this experience, I continued to drink and use drugs. When I was 22 years old, I went fishing one day with my friend in the Miramichi River. It was a very hot summer day. As usual we were both very drunk, and he fell asleep in the boat. Somehow in my drunken state, I fell overboard and got tangled in the fishnet under the boat. I couldn't get loose. I felt a sense of panic and fear that this time no one would help me, and I'd drown. This time I would really die.

But like when I was sixteen, I found myself again drawn down a long tunnel. It was a wonderful feeling going through it again and looking up and seeing the light ahead. When I got to the top, the light was bright, but it was so peaceful and loving. This time the light didn't blind or hurt my eyes. It was amazing. Then I found myself on a cloud. It moved toward a doorway where my grandparents were standing. There was a teepee, some animals and a river. It was such a beautiful place with meadows and valleys.

As I walked in, I thought how much I wanted to stay there with my ancestors. Then my grandfather spoke to me in my language: "My grandson, you must go back because you have work to do for the people and for the earth. Soon you will be given some sacred powers to help in your work." I remember saying as I started to walk away, "I don't want to go back." But he told me again that I must go back because of the work I had to do.

After I traveled back through the tunnel, I found I was no longer in the water or caught in the fishnet. I was on the boat. My friend was still passed out, and there was no one else around. That shook me up, and I began to think that there might be a Creator out there who was watching over me. It was much later that I understood that we really are watched over by the Great Spirit every day of our lives, no matter what or where we are.

Until I was 24, I continued to drink anything I could get my hands on that had alcohol in it — shaving lotion, rubbing alcohol, perfume, Lysol, melted shoe polish. I drank because of the pain and the scars that were left on me. I wanted to forget the shame from the abuses that had happened. I became known as the "reserve drunk." I suffered serious heart problems, and I even used prescription drugs. I was a disgrace and embarrassment to my family, my people, to the whole Miramichi people and to myself.

One day as I was coming out of an alcoholic fit, I was very hung over. I had been terribly sick all day. In fact I almost had the DTs (delirium tremens). My sister asked me to take care of her daughter, my niece Oasaweg, while she went to the store to get groceries. I asked her to bring me back a bottle of shaving lotion or Lysol or anything to calm my nerves.

My niece and I went for a walk because I couldn't stay still in the house. We went toward the river right where the Mother Earth Lodge stands today. As we walked, I fell to the ground and started shaking with the cold sweats, nausea, everything. I wanted a drink so badly. I felt very weak, and I started to cry. My niece kept asking me, "What's wrong, uncle? Are you all right?" I looked up at her and said, "I am so sick. And I am so sick and tired of being sick and tired. All this alcohol and drinking and stuff are killing me." She looked me straight in the eye and said, "Uncle, why don't you just pray?"

So at that very moment I did. I asked the Great Spirit to give me the help I needed. From the tip of my toes to the top of my head, a warm feeling started coming over me. My whole body began to tingle. When I looked up at the sky, I saw an eagle above us. It circled around four times before it flew west. When I stood up, I felt like something had been lifted from my soul. And I didn't have the terrible craving for alcohol.

We walked back to the house just as my sister returned. She wasn't able to find any rubbing alcohol or Lysol or anything to help me. I told her it was okay because I didn't need it. She looked at me with great surprise, because she knew I was a chronic alcoholic who would drink anything to keep my nerves calm. She asked if I was sure I didn't need something. I said I didn't. From that day on I never touched a drink. And now it's already many years later. Talk about a blessing from the Great Spirit!

The next day I left the reservation and started traveling. I went to Prince Edward Island to visit my brother George Paul. He too had been an alcoholic — as were all my brothers and sisters. But eventually every one of us stopped drinking and got on with our spiritual lives.

George Paul was conducting sweat lodge ceremonies on Prince Edward Island. The Mi'Kmaq use sweat lodges to purify themselves from moral, spiritual or physical weaknesses. The hot stones in the center symbolize the presence of our ancestors, and during the ceremony we can call on them for spiritual help. Water is poured over the hot rocks as a symbol of life and of cleanliness. For example, if the Spirit of the Bear appears during a sweat, it is a symbol of strength, fortitude and endurance.

For about a year I stayed with George Paul and his wife. As my older brother, he really took me under his wing, gave me a lot of support and nourishment, and was very inspirational to me. He helped guide me toward my native spirituality — what I describe as respect for all living things: Mother Earth, food, relatives, all peoples of the human race.

One day George Paul gave me my first sacred pipe. I had gone to numerous ceremonies and sweats and was clearly working on getting my act together. When he gave me that pipe, he said, "May the pipe bring you strength, knowledge and wisdom."

While I lived on Prince Edward Island, I did a mini naming ceremony and received my Mi'Kmaq spirit name, Spotted Eagle Boy. It's important that your spirit name and your life walk together in honor. When you have a spirit name, it is expected that you carry it with respect. The spotted eagle is a holy or sacred bird that sits next to the Creator. From the minute I was named Spotted Eagle Boy, I knew I must walk the talk. I had to keep myself clean and sober. There could be no room in my life for alcohol or drugs. A great responsibility was placed on me when I was given such a powerful name.

While I was staying with George Paul, I met a blind Mi'Kmaq medicine man from a Nova Scotia reserve. He told me the Great Spirit had given me a gift and it was time that I put it to work. He asked me to travel with him. So we traveled for several months and he taught me many things.

One day when we were doing ceremonies for elderly people in Alberta, he told me it was time for me to learn how to fly on my own —

as the eagle does. So he went home, and I continued doing ceremonies. After some time I hitchhiked to Montana, where I hopped on a freight train and rode the rails. Wherever I went, I felt the Spirit's sense of freedom and power. I had no fear and no doubts because of the Presence that was around me.

Jerome Four Star, a Sioux medicine man, picked me up when I was hitchhiking one day. He took me to his home in Wolf Point, Montana. Not long after I arrived, Jerome said, "You should go back and get your sacred pipe." Two weeks earlier I had left my pipe in my luggage on the floor of a bus depot in Great Falls, Montana. I didn't even put it in a locker. I don't know how he knew my pipe was there, because I didn't tell him. But this guy was a medicine man who worked with Spirits, and they probably told on me! He gave me $10 for coffee and meals. I was to come back with my pipe. It would take a couple of days to get to Great Falls.

So I hitchhiked and eventually arrived at the bus depot, and my duffel bag was still sitting on the floor where I left it two weeks before. I picked up my bag and started back to Jerome's place. Right then I knew my life was going to be a wonderful journey.

I hopped on a freight train and rode to Wolf Point. Riding the rails was a beautiful experience. Montana is what I call big-sky country. From the top of the train, I could look around and see how great and beautiful the land and the sky are. I saw thousands of birds and deer and horses. I had an incredible sense of freedom — even during the times when I got really hungry or thirsty with the wind blowing hard on me.

When I arrived back at Jerome's place, he said to me, "I'm adopting you as my grandson. Grandson, you are now my grandson. And now I'm going to teach you the ways that will help people as you go on your journey." So for the next two and a half years I stayed with Jerome and went to ceremonies with him. He taught me what would happen when I went on a vision quest and how to prepare for it.

One cloudy day Jerome took me high up on a mountain and told me he was going to leave me there for four days. At the top, he said:

"Grandson, I want you to take out your pipe and fill it. Then you must call the eagle, and I want to see it." He told me how to concentrate on calling the eagle in my prayer. I was not to allow my mind to wander. As I filled my pipe and prayed hard, I asked the spotted eagle to join me in this sacred ceremony. Finally Jerome tapped me on my shoulder and told me to look up. To my great surprise I saw the eagle flying in the sky. I started to cry. "Well, grandson, now I must go," he said. And he walked down the mountain.

With great feelings in my heart, I sat alone on the big mountain. Even though it was totally unknown to me, I felt no fear. I saw no houses or people anywhere on the mountain. Even when it grew darker and colder, I still was not afraid. I sat there with my pipe as everything became pitch dark black. I could not see my hand in front of me. I remembered the words of the song "I've Got to Walk This Lonesome Valley." I sat there in the darkness and felt the beauty of it. I heard the animals make their ceremonies in the night. As the sun came up early the next morning, I heard the birds singing and heard everything come alive. It was amazing. I didn't sleep at all that first night.

On the second day, it rained hard all day, and in the evening it started to hail. It got very windy and cold. I was only wearing my moccasins, my sun dance skirt and a blanket. I held on to my pipe and prayed, which is what saved me and kept me warm. I forgot about myself as I prayed for other people — the children who were suffering and starving, the elderly. I prayed for the animals and Mother Earth. I had a lot of time to pray because I was there for four days with no food and no water.

The third night the spirits came and told me that sometime in the future I would be given knowledge, wisdom and sacred gifts and I would be told how to use them. On the evening of the fourth day, I had a vision about a sacred tree and a man who presented a knife to me.

The next day Jerome came to get me, and we went down the mountain to his place. He had me drink some special medicine. Then we went to another place, where I saw a group of men carefully carrying a big 40-foot-long aspen tree, which was not to touch the ground. A man gave me a knife and told me I should carve the thunderbolt on the tree. With the branches I was to make a thunderbird nest. After I did that, the tree was set up in a hole that had been dug about six feet deep. The rain dance would take place around the tree.

I was to dance because I was suffering for my people. I would sacrifice myself for my loved ones. Sage was wrapped around my wrists, my ankles and my head as rain dance wreaths. Two piercing sticks carved from white willow were stuck deep into the flesh on my chest. A rope was tied from the tree to the two sticks on both sides of my chest. I was supposed to keep the rope tight by pulling back from the tree as I danced. But the flesh was not to break or be torn away from my chest during my dance. For four days I would dance without food or water.

During the afternoons we sat down and smoked our pipes. Even if it was 100 degrees in the sun, we did not sit in the shade and had no water. I could only stop and lie down in the evening, but I was still connected to the tree because it was part of the ceremony.

Doing the rain dance was one of the greatest things in my life. Having come out of an alcoholic place and knowing very little about spiritual things, it was a wonderful experience for me, and I appreciated every minute. During the dance I didn't experience any physical pain, but I felt that my spiritual life was becoming very powerful. I didn't think about food or water, because I had gone beyond physical needs into a spiritual state where food and water no longer mattered. I was in a beautiful space of total trust. Nothing could hurt me. It was a special healing experience.

While I danced, I looked at the sacred tree, and I began to see visions of the Spirits coming out of it. The Spirits talk to you not in words but in a way that you can understand, because your mind and body are clear of poisons and toxins. And your heart and spirit are so open that you can hear and understand them. That's what happens when you dance or fast. It's a great way to connect to the Great Spirit.

The elders had taught me that the rain dance was done to call upon the Thunder Beings that bring the rain and water to nourish the animals and all of nature. In some tribes the Thunder Beings are called sacred clowns, and they are very powerful healers. People who receive spirits from them are capable of healing people, and they have great powers.

The next year was a very difficult year for the Mi'Kmaqs. I kept in contact with the people in Red Bank, so I knew there were a lot of problems among the people, like alcoholism and drug use. My people were suffering.

So when Jerome took me back up the mountain for my vision quest the next year, I knew I needed to do something for my people. I wanted to help them with their pain, guilt and shame. As I stayed on the mountain those four days and nights, I really prayed about that. I asked the Great Spirit what I could do and how I could help make things better for the Mi'Kmaq people.

On my last night on the mountain as I sat praying for a vision for my people, I saw a beautiful building made from logs. It was sitting on a hill overlooking the Miramichi River. There were many activities, dances and ceremonies going on in the building, and lots of people were using it — from children to elders. I was so excited to see all the possibilities. I saw that the building was to be used as a healing place for people who would come to receive comfort, guidance, healing and spiritual food. It would serve like a mother who feeds her children. The place was to be the Mother Earth Lodge, and it would especially help people who suffered from drug and alcohol addiction. But it would be more than a rehabilitation center; it would be a spiritual center open to all peoples of all races and cultures — not just the native people living at Red Bank First Nation.

When I came down the mountain after my vision quest, I told my adopted grandfather what I had seen and what the Great Spirit had told me to do. He said it was a wonderful idea and that the Great Spirit does not lie. He told me that when you are given a vision about what you ought to do with your life, it is expected that you will follow through with it. If you don't, you would be breaking your personal commitment to the Great Spirit. So after reflecting on my vision quest, I began to talk about my vision with people. Many liked the idea and were supportive of it.

I only stayed in Montana a little longer with my adopted grandfather Jerome. Then I moved on to South Dakota, Texas and Minnesota, where I had many more wonderful experiences teaching native culture and ceremonies. In Philadelphia I tried to help kids who were selling themselves for money and using drugs and alcohol. When I was invited to go to New York, I realized that I was definitely moving back in the direction of my home in Canada.

My life has been filled with special blessings and fantastic experiences that have given me opportunities to learn. I was frequently given spiritual awakenings and inner peace. I also met a lot of great people along the way and told them about the Mother Earth Lodge. Some of them offered to help support the costs of building it.

After seven years of traveling, I headed back home at last. I was only 25 years old when I left home and started my spiritual journey. I was 32 when I arrived back in Red Bank. I had been a chronic alcoholic and the reserve drunk when I left. I was a nobody. I was always on the street, I was dirty, my hair was messy and I never had on clean clothes. I was drunk all the time. I stole things to get money to get drunk. I lied to get drunk. I sold anything to get drunk. That's the kind of spirit that had taken over my mind, body and soul. Because I was already drinking at the age of nine and was an alcoholic by age fourteen, that was how people knew me. But I came out of all of that at the age of 25, and my whole life turned around. I had gotten a second chance in life — a new beginning.

When I first arrived back home, people couldn't believe it was me. They kept saying things like, "Tulley, is that you?" They told me how good I looked. Before I left home, I was really skinny. I had no nourishment in me because I wasn't eating. My eyes were sunk in my head from all the alcohol. But when I came back home, I was a healthy, nourished, longhaired man. And I spoke our language well. Before I left, I couldn't speak it at all because of my experiences at the residential school.

By the time I returned to the Red Bank Reserve, I had regained my strength, my sight, my language, my culture. And I had recovered my spirit and my spirituality. What a wonderful way of waking up to a new life and to all that I had missed out on before! There were so many powerful elders, medicine people and others who helped give me power and healing along the way.

As I shared my vision and stories with my people, they believed me. Many of the people including the leaders and the elders had gone through a lot of hardship and suffering themselves, so they were open to what I said and very supportive of my vision.

Soon we started planning the building of the Mother Earth Lodge. After talking with the leaders in the community, we obtained a Certificate of Propriety for three acres of land from the Department of Indian Affairs in 1992. Shortly after that we started the foundation of the building, but we didn't have enough money for what we hoped to build. So I went back on the road to do more fund-raising. Finally, after nearly four years, we completed the Mother Earth Lodge.

Unfortunately on the day of its grand opening, the Mother Earth Lodge burned down to the ground at four in the morning. When I saw what had happened, I couldn't believe it. There was so much pain and disappointment. I felt almost defeated. What had happened to the wonderful vision I had dreamed on my vision quest?

Almost 3,000 people came to the grand opening dedication, and all they saw were the remains of the charred building. There was great sadness in everyone's hearts. I cried for almost four days — it took me that long to come out of the pain and sorrow of that awful loss.

After that I prayed to the Great Spirit for guidance and was told to rebuild the lodge on the same place — only the new one was to be bigger because it could help more people. We got a bulldozer and leveled the ground; we would build on the ashes of the first lodge. Then we went right to work building a second lodge — a bigger and better one.

It only took us four months to build the new lodge. Today there are so many things going on in the lodge, like cultural activities, all kinds of workshops, Alcoholics Anonymous meetings, spiritual talking circles, women's talking circles, talks about the medicine wheel and healing. It's going full-blast with a staff and board of directors, and it's incorporated.

Looking back, I would say that the lowest time in my life happened when I was taken away from my parents as a small child and placed in the Indian residential school. Because of that, I never got my parents' love and affection when I needed it. It was taken away from me when I was very young. And I lost my innocence.

It's easy to understand why I started to become bitter toward white people. It felt like they were trying to take our spirit and our land and to kill our buffalo. So why do native people forgive them so easily? It is because of the teachings from the Great Spirit. I believe those teachings are in our blood, in our hearts and in our spirits. I believe one day the white people will see and understand that what they did was wrong. So in spite of everything that has happened, we must forgive them and work with them.

If we forgive, we can continue to work for the Great Spirit, and there will be no blockage and no hatred as we work. We can work with a clear mind and a clear spirit. If we walk around with hatred in our heart, we are just passing that on to innocent children or people. After we forgive, we can let the Great Spirit take care of what they've done.

Certainly no one forces me to walk the clean and sober path. I must do that myself. Native spirituality requires those who are involved with sacred things like spiritual leadership and spiritual healing to be positive role models for others. So I must always begin with myself in a spiritual cleansing.

Sometimes it's difficult to face ourselves, and it hurts when we see the harm and pain we have caused ourselves and others over the years. Although it's hard to do, once we have really faced ourselves we are given many insights into our own Walk of Life.

When I work with people who have had so much taken away from them, I tell them that the Great Spirit works in mysterious and wonderful ways. Lots of times people are so in doubt and so in fear.

But I try to walk with them by telling them the stories of my life, where I've been, what I went through and how I survived by the power of the Great Spirit and with the support of all the people who helped me.

The Great Spirit has a plan and a lot of ideas for all of us in this world. Often we have doubts or fears or we forget that the Great Spirit exists and protects us. Sometimes when we are on a spiritual path, we run into what I call "dry faith," where we sort of lose contact with the Spirit. We can become doubtful or bitter or less compassionate and understanding.

But somewhere along the road something happens, and the Spirit reappears and strengthens our faith and our belief. We can't compare this to normal things that happen in our lives. With spirituality we may not understand it very well, but we'll know it is good and from the other side.

Yes, there is always hope, and there is always prayer. There is always something good — just look for it and you can find it. You can get out of a negative place and step into another place of healing, goodness and wellness.

A very good vision is needed for life, and the man who has it must follow it — as the eagle seeks the deepest blue of the sky.

— Chief Crazy Horse

Listening to Tulley recount the story of his terrible losses, abuses and addictions, I marveled that he had survived and somehow become a role model for others. He had been deeply wounded. But out of pain and suffering, "healing" can occur.

Many healing journeys are jump-started when we "hit bottom." This can be true for individuals, families, communities, even nations. Sometimes, like Tulley, we may be blessed with the wisdom and guidance of caring people who help us forgive, reclaim our authentic selves and discover what we are meant to do. As is often true, healing can lead to a deeper sense of belonging, service and vocation.

Tulley Spotted Eagle Boy's story teaches us if brokenness or anger go unhealed, they can become another toxic poison to ourselves, our society, the environment and the world. Practicing forgiveness and clearing hatred from our hearts makes room for the "Great Spirit" to work hope-filled miracles in our lives. And we may feel empowered to reach out and gain a vision of service to our communities and the larger world as instruments of healing and reconciliation.

Perhaps the greatest gift Tulley gives to us is the value of sharing our honest stories with those who are filled with fear, doubt and pain, with those who are in need of healing. Storytelling has always been an important part of native spirituality and life. Stories of hurt, grief, suffering, renewal and rebirth require close listening and attention. We need to hold them in our hearts and in our memory for sharing with others.

We all have stories to tell, stories that will provide wisdom along the journey of life to each other and to the generations to come. What better gift can we give each other than the open and honest truth about our human endeavors. Tulley's and our stories of adversities and triumphs can help put our history into a clearer perspective. In the process, we may grow wiser, more patient and more connected to each other and the earth.

As Rumi wrote: "But don't be satisfied with stories, how things have gone with others. Unfold your own myth, without complicated explanation, so everyone will understand the passage, 'We have opened you.'"

ALAN AND JENNY

Towers of Faith

*I told them how afraid I had been when I first came to this white parish.
I felt their genuine acceptance of me and Jenny,
and I sensed my deep wounds were being cleansed.* – Alan

*We couldn't figure out what was going on.
I was trying to avoid middle-aged white women, and they seemed drawn
to me. I began to think God was sending angels into my life.* – Jenny

*One day, you will look back and understand why God allowed you
to have this pain. You will be called to speak to people who are in pain.
Until you stop questioning why this is happening, you will not experience
release and healing.* – Archbishop Desmond Tutu

In the mid-1970s I became friends with people involved in the anti-*apartheid* movement in South Africa, several of whom were living in exile at the time. They wove a tale of brutality about the South African *apartheid* regime and its racist exploitations. We acknowledged that healing from such outrageous injustices was painful, drawn-out and difficult. Often my friends spoke of their admiration for the courageous contributions of the imprisoned Nelson Mandela and of a gutsy and articulate Anglican priest, Desmond Tutu, who seemed fearless as he spoke out against the wrongs and inequities in the country.

One night as I was attending a class at the St. Luke's School for Healing in Connecticut, Alan and Jenny Dennis, a handsome young couple from South Africa, were introduced as the guest speakers for the evening. They spoke with sadness and compassion about the unjust discrimination and obstacles imposed on them as so-called "colored people" living under apartheid.

Jenny

I grew up in Crawford, a suburb of Cape Town where only colored people lived. In South Africa, if you were colored, you were not white nor were you black; you were a "mixed breed." My paternal grandfather was Italian, my maternal grandmother was British, and their spouses were both colored. By the age of 16, everyone had to carry a book with an ID number indicating whether we were black, white, colored or Asian.

Sometimes when I rode the bus to greater Cape Town and passed the white schools, I could see their sports facilities were much better than ours. I began to realize there was a big difference in the way we were treated. By grade seven, I knew I was judged a lesser being because of the color of my skin.

On Independence Day, my school had a special flag-raising ceremony. When I was in the first grade, I was chosen to raise the flag, which made my dad proud. But when I was supposed to raise the flag in grade seven as the prefect of the school, I no longer felt the South African flag was part of my country. So I refused to do it. My father, who had very strong opinions about loyalty to one's country, had taken the day off for the event. He was really angry at me. "But, Daddy," I cried. "How can I do this if I don't believe in it?" My father stared at me and then said, "Jenny, if you believe you shouldn't do this, then it's fine."

Sadly, three months later my father died suddenly. I was only thirteen. For a long time I wished I had raised that flag to make him proud. I would have if I had known he would soon die. I was filled with grief and was angry with the government that had caused me to inflict pain on my father. I was 32 before I finally realized that my dad had forgiven me but I needed to forgive myself.

Whenever my British grandmother and I took the bus to greater Cape Town, we had to climb the steep stairs to the colored section, even though she had trouble with her legs. Once she fell going down the stairs. The conductor rushed to her. When he saw her blonde hair and blue eyes, he asked, "Why were *you* sitting upstairs?" She replied, "I was with my granddaughter." He was reaching out to help her, but when he saw me he said, "Then you can get up by yourself." He left my grandmother with her legs bleeding lying on the floor. "Someone please help my granny," I cried. But the white people just turned their heads away. As we got off the bus, I told my grandmother I hated them. "No, Jenny," she said, "the only way to stop this is to love them."

Alan

When I grew up, my mother often pleaded with me not to get involved in political things. Although it was painful for her, she also said, "You have to do what you have to do." My father and some of his friends participated in demonstrations at an early age. Some of them became leading attorneys and writers who later were imprisoned or in exile.

During my last years of high school, people were being uprooted and forced to move from their communities because of the Group Areas Act, which decreed that whites, blacks and coloreds could only live in certain areas. It was an explosive time. In 1972, when I was a junior, I was involved in establishing a newspaper: *Cry Out*. We wanted to say what we needed to say. I had to get permission from the vice-headmaster. Initially there was a lot of opposition.

The paper created opportunities to interact with the local black high school and community. Of course, young people meeting together was against government policy and was considered dangerous. In my senior year during a meeting with black students, the Security Police busted the meeting and threw us in prison for the weekend. The government did not want people interacting. *Apartheid* was about setting people apart, so heavy scare tactics were applied. That experience showed the faculty that we were ready to make sacrifices the older generation wasn't, and they approved the paper.

Being in prison was a pivotal experience for me. I had more chances to interact with blacks. I saw they were more deprived of education than I was and my humble home was a castle as compared to many of theirs.

In the mid-'70s, many people suddenly disappeared. The Internal Security Act 29 had been implemented: detention without trial for 90 days. In 1976, children in Soweto, a large black Johannesburg suburb, were protesting against being taught in Afrikaans, which was not their native language and was considered the language of the oppressor. On June 16, as thousands of children held a protest march, the police shot directly into the crowd, killing hundreds. That event mobilized children throughout the country.

After I completed my studies at the Anglican seminary of St. Peter's College in 1978, things drastically changed for me. The Archbishop assigned me to one of the wealthiest white parishes in the country, the first appointment across the color line. After Soweto, I wanted to work in township parishes, where the action was. My friends were going to township parishes in colored areas involved with suffering, violence and imprisonment. Because I was going to a plush, white parish, I was immediately ostracized. I felt betrayed and angry.

When I asked the Archbishop if my appointment could be changed, he explained: "This is a way to start somewhere." He had decided to take action while there was pressure in the country. Placing me, who didn't look black or very colored, in a white parish would be more acceptable than an African black. At least the Archbishop was honest about attempting to make changes. Although ambivalent, I trusted God had a hand in this. Perhaps I was to be a bridge builder.

Because of the Group Areas Act, I was told that people of color employed by the church required permits to live on the property. I told the rector, "I won't apply for a permit." Eventually I lived there without a permit. I understood the possible consequences: The police could arrest me for transgressing the Group Areas Act, and I could be put in prison for 30 days without trial.

At first, it didn't register with all of the parishioners who I was. Some people were patronizing to me, but those in leadership positions were generally supportive. I hung onto the belief that I'd been sent there for a reason and couldn't leave without making some difference.

I lived in the house for four months before Jenny and I were married. She often said that when the parishioners saw her, they finally knew who I was. Some of my anger was caused by the rejection Jenny experienced. I had problems with people accepting me because I was a priest while at the same time behaving so nastily toward Jenny. Her pain affected both of us.

Meanwhile, my colleagues thought I was having a great holiday in a lovely white parish while they were working in the townships where things were tough. When I saw them at conferences, I was simply ignored. It was more than a white-black issue; it was rejection by my own people.

Jenny

Before we were married, I wasn't afraid of moving to Alan's church or of being rejected. On the first Sunday after we were married, I sat in the front pew of the church with the other clergy wives. It was then that the people realized I was Alan's wife. I could see that they were shocked. I had been so naïve, thinking people would accept me. People greeted me at church, but if I met them on the street or in shops, they walked right by, ignoring me completely.

One day as I was gardening, I heard a man shout, "Hey, you!" I didn't think he meant me. "Hey, you. I'm speaking to *you*." I asked if he was talking to me. "Yes," he said. "Is your boss, Father Dennis, at home?" Obviously he assumed I was the maid. I invited him in, stood in the passageway, and shouted, "Darling, there's a gentleman here to see you." Of course, "darling" came. Unfortunately, this kind of thing put a strain on our relationship. Sometimes I blamed Alan for getting us into the mess. I didn't always verbalize it, but it would boil inside me. Alan knew how I felt, and it hurt him too.

While I was pregnant with Jill, I became friends with some young mothers from the church. After she was born, we formed a nursery in our home. The mothers took turns caring for the babies during church services. One Sunday I was receiving babies and visiting with my friends when a beautifully dressed woman walked up. "I'm here to see Father Dennis's wife," she said. "He has been wonderful to my family. We'd like to give their new baby a gift." Smiling, I said, "Thank you. I'm his wife. The baby is inside." She looked stunned. "*You're* his wife?" Before I could say anything, she threw the gift at my feet and walked away. I stood there in shock, humiliated in front of my friends.

Alan was furious. We talked about leaving the church, but he still believed God had called him there. After that I cut myself off from almost everyone, especially middle-aged, white women. Whenever anyone got near Jill, I protected her fiercely, like a lioness with her cub. People could do things to me, but they didn't dare touch my child.

So Alan's job became *his* job alone. I only talked with Alan about what I was going through, another burden for him. He had to serve as priest to people who were hurting his wife.

Alan

In 1980 the Archbishop gave me a scholarship to study pastoral clinical education in Toronto. Being in Canada was healing for us. One day as we walked toward the entrance of a ferryboat, we looked for signs indicating which turnstile non-whites were allowed to use. After doing that all our lives, it was an instinctive thing. When we realized there were no signs to tell us which turnstile we couldn't use, we started laughing. "You know what," I shouted, "we're free!"

That was the beginning of our freedom from political and emotional oppression, from gates we weren't allowed to go through and from doors that had turned us away. We felt a new release and knew we wanted to be free. Jenny didn't need to be in her cocoon anymore; she was ready to break out. We went to every place where there were no signs to block us: restaurants, the post office, trains, everywhere. We energized ourselves in preparation for going back home.

Upon our return to South Africa we were assigned to a large colored parish in Grassy Park and later to Macassar, a semi-rural colored parish where most of the people had been displaced from their homes as a result of the Group Areas Act. Our challenge was to support and build up the community.

When our daughter Jill was five, she performed at an Eistedfodd, a competition for ballet schools. We left her at the dressing room and went to the hall to find seats. Unbeknownst to us, Jill was not allowed in the dressing room because she was "beige." She was sent to a dirty toilet to put on her costume. During the performance, Jill didn't do well. We thought she was probably just nervous.

On the way home, she asked, "Mommy and Daddy, why am I beige?" At first we thought it was funny and asked her where she had gotten such an idea. She explained how the mothers had forced her to change in the toilet because of her color.

Jenny

We were angry and saddened by this terrible episode. We felt awful that we had been sitting in the auditorium while she was undergoing such humiliation. At home Jill climbed on her bed and clutched her oldest rag doll. Although the doll had no clothes and very little hair, Jill never allowed us to get rid of it.

I told Jill to stand beside me in front of the mirror. "What do you see?" I asked. "I see you and me," she answered. "What else?" She pointed to her tattered doll. "Would you like to get rid of it?" I asked. She stared at me. "No, it's my favorite doll." I pointed out that the doll was dirty, barely had any hair, and had no clothes. "But it's my doll," she protested. "God's just like you with your doll," I explained. "No matter what you do, no matter what you look like, no matter who you are, God loves you — as much as you love this doll. And God doesn't judge you by the color of your skin." Jill's little face brightened up. I think she began to understand.

Alan

Shortly after Jill's experience at the Eistedfodd, we heard about a flag raising ceremony at her school. We explained how the raising of the flag represented a validation of oppression, like what had happened when she had been called beige. So she would not participate in that, but would go to school late that day. It was our way of protesting against the government and refusing to allow ourselves to be mistreated.

Later I drove Jill to school. As she got out of the car, some kids asked her why she was late. With her hands on her hips, she boldly declared, "Because I'm protesting the South African Government." From her little body came such big ideas. It was the beginning of her healing process.

Since English was the language used in our home, we wanted Jill to attend an English-speaking school. So we drove her to a private school in Somerset West. However, by the time she was in the second grade, the costs were getting beyond us. We were told there was an Anglican girls' school that had been founded to accommodate clergy children. No clergy child would be rejected, and we would get a discount on the tuition. When I called for an appointment, the headmaster said they would welcome Jill as a student.

At the school, one of the staff told us the school was going through a down time and it would be good to have Jill. However, as soon as we entered the white headmaster's office and he saw Jenny's face, he started telling us that the school was full and there was no room for Jill. He assured us her name would be on the waiting list.

We were furious. "You're refusing our daughter entrance because we're not white." He kept saying, "No, the school is full, but her name is on the wait list." Finally I said, "I don't believe you. Before we get angrier, it's better for us to leave your office."

When we got in our car, we were both shaking with anger. I thought about calling Archbishop Desmond Tutu, my Archbishop at the time, and telling him what had happened. I decided to wait and let things cool down.

A few days later, I received a call from the Archbishop's office. We suspected it might be about a new parish. Jenny said, "If this is an offer, there are two things to remember: It must not be a white parish and it's got to be a small house."

At the Archbishop's office, as soon as I was told I had done a lot of bridge building, I started feeling nervous. I was concerned where I might be sent. The offer was an upper class, 90 percent white parish at the foot of Table Mountain, one of the most expensive areas of Cape Town. At the age of 34, I was to be the first non-white rector of that church. The assignment included a huge house, bigger than anything we had lived in, with many bedrooms and a master bedroom large enough to play badminton. With the parish came another surprise: I would be chaplain to the school where Jill had been rejected. I had not yet told the Archbishop what had happened at the school. Suddenly the whole picture had flipped around. Right then I knew God has a sense of humor.

Jenny

When Alan returned, I heard the car pull up and heard him go into his office and close the door. I thought: "He's obviously disappointed." So I gave him time. Finally Alan told me he had been offered a parish in Cape Town. And there were two more things: One was a very big house. "I guess I can handle that," I laughed. "What's the other thing?" I wasn't prepared for: "It's a white church." I threw the plate I was holding onto the floor and cried, "There's no way I'll go to a white church." I was furious with God. I had tried hard to be supportive of Alan, to go wherever he was called, and here God was doing this to me — again.

After that I tried to convince God that this parish was not the place where we should go. I assumed Alan wanted to go, and I felt I wasn't as important to him as God. Therefore, God was causing this rift and taking my husband away from me.

A few weeks later I told Alan I was willing to look at the church. So we walked past the huge house. Several days before Alan was to give his decision, we were driving to a meeting. Suddenly I thought I heard the words, "Go, and the Lord said go." As we drove on, I kept hearing that. Then I said, "And the Lord said go." I told Alan, "That's not me. I don't want to go." I knew I was having a battle with myself. Finally I said, "Okay, I'll go, but only out of obedience. I don't know why God wants me to go, but I will."

Alan

As chaplain of the school I phoned the headmaster, who had forgotten who I was. But when I walked into his office, he turned gray. The first words out of his mouth were, "Reverend Dennis, your daughter is most welcome to this school." It's rare that I want to pull rank, but that day I said, "Of course, my daughter will be here because I'm the chaplain of the school. I have something else to say: Either you leave or I leave, and since I've just come I'm not leaving." He replied, "Tomorrow I will hand in my resignation."

On February 11, 1990, I was instituted as rector of the parish at three o'clock, the exact hour and day that Nelson Mandela was freed from prison and made his freedom speech in Cape Town. The country was definitely in a healing mode.

When we first arrived, the vestry arranged a welcoming barbecue party, where a senior member pulled me aside and asked: "I just want to know if this is one of the Archbishop's political moves?" I knew I shouldn't get into that with him, so I answered, "We'll have to see." He replied, "Yes, we'll have to see."

About six months later at one of the vestry meetings, the same man announced he had something urgent to say. He insisted it be on the agenda. He began by confessing he had thought my appointment was a political move, and he reminded others that they too had expressed the same concern. "So tonight," he said, as tears filled his eyes, "I want to publicly apologize to Alan. We were quick to judge. Now we've had six months together, and we know this is God's will working in our lives. I want every one in this room to say what they need to say."

Initially I was overwhelmed and didn't say a word. I listened to each person speak and cried with them. Then I told them what I had felt when I first came to this white parish. Finally we held hands and prayed together. I sensed their genuine acceptance of me and of Jenny. Everything that needed to be said was said that night, and I realized my deep wounds were being cleansed with a kind of healing balm.

After that I began to understand where the Archbishop had been going with this. In the struggle for liberty and peace in our country, one had to do such things. This was about God, about the church, about building bridges and helping to heal our wounded nation. So if I was being asked to do this, then I needed to be obedient and open. My colleagues and friends who had distanced themselves from me also realized that this was about a new South Africa and a call to heal and make whole.

Next door to our church was a Dutch Reformed Church, the Afrikaans-speaking State Church. When I was in seminary, another student and I had visited one of these churches. Although we were in the back, somebody noticed us and removed us. We protested, saying we had come to worship, but the man pushed us out. The incident made me bitter and angry toward that church.

Shortly after I started working in the parish, a new minister arrived at the neighboring church. Although I knew I should welcome him, the painful memory of my humiliating experience still haunted me. Finally I walked over to the parish house and introduced myself. Eventually we became friends, and the two congregations developed a relationship.

Later my friend invited me to preach in his church. He suggested the time was right. Initially I refused, afraid that preaching there would be too difficult for me. Finally I went and preached a sermon about how God can change our lives. From then on people began greeting me on the streets.

Jenny

After we had been in the white parish for about four years, Alan and I did a sermon together about grace and healing. I spoke about the pain and rejection at our first white church. I compared that to the experience of being in this parish where people were supportive and how healing that was. I could be with white people again. Many people said my story made them want to be with people of other colors. After 15 years, Alan and I were coming around full circle, and we began to realize that healing was a two-way street.

Whenever we led Marriage Encounter Weekends (a program for married couples wanting to enrich their marriage), we openly shared information about the rejections we had experienced and how we tried to be barrier breakers and bridge builders. At the end of each session, at least one middle-aged white woman would hug and thank me. Usually it would be the one woman I had picked out of the group as a serious racist. We couldn't figure out what was going on. I was trying to avoid middle-aged white women, and they seemed drawn to me. I began to think God was sending angels into my life who were helping heal my past wounds.

In 1994, we hosted an international Marriage Encounter convention in Cape Town. Some American couples talked about "The Engaged Workshop," a pre-marital program that was run by a couple in Connecticut. We were interested in this program because it seemed inclusive enough to be beneficial for people in South Africa, no matter what their religion: Hindu, Jew, Muslim, Christian.

Later that year my back was seriously reinjured in an automobile accident. Seven years earlier I had had extensive surgery on it. On July

29, an orthopedic surgeon informed me that there was nothing more that could be done for me because the risks were too great of my becoming paralyzed. I had been in bed for weeks and could barely walk. The pain was so excruciating that I was planning to start a pain management program to learn how to adapt to this way of living. I was depressed and wondered what I would do with the rest of my life.

That evening when the phone rang, I heard Alan exclaim, "That's great, but I'm not sure we'll be able to come." We had been invited to the States to participate in the Connecticut training workshop in September. They would pay for one ticket if we could pay for the other. "If God wants us to go," I said, "He will heal my back."

Alan

We knew we couldn't afford airfare to New York. So if we were to go, God not only had to heal Jenny's back but also provide us with the money. We thought the only person who might be willing to assist us was Archbishop Desmond Tutu. He had always been keen on international activities and encouraged a broad worldview for clergy and people in his Diocese. He was also our Diocesan Bishop and knew us well. When Jenny had back surgery in 1987, he often visited her in our home.

We were aware that the Archbishop was very busy so I called his chaplain, a friend of mine, to ask if it would be possible to get an appointment with him. My friend called that evening to tell us we had one the next Wednesday afternoon.

We carefully got Jenny into the car on Wednesday. She had not been out of bed for a month.

Jenny

At his office, the Archbishop asked: "Jenny, how is your back?" "Father, you don't want to know," I answered. "I feel depressed and have a lot of pain. Why am I praying and not being healed? I must have done something very wrong in my life, and God is punishing me. Perhaps I have sinned so much that He isn't able to heal me."

I'll never forget what he said. "Jenny, then Jesus must have been the greatest sinner of all, because no one suffered more than He did. What you need to do, my daughter, is give thanks for what God has given you. And you need to embrace this pain. There may be a reason for it. You need to give it to God and leave it with Him."

For a moment I just stared at him as I thought about those words. He went on: "One day you will look back on this experience and understand why you have this pain. You will be called to speak to people who are in pain, and you can tell them you've been there. Embrace that pain and then give it back to God. Until you can accept this and stop questioning why it is happening to you, you will not experience release and healing."

Then he laid his hands on me and prayed. After he said "Amen," he ruffled my hair and turned to Alan. "Now I hear you guys want to go to America."

Alan

We had been told we had 20 minutes with the Archbishop. By the time he turned to me, we had already been there 40 minutes. Talk about "hands on" pastoral care: In front of my eyes I watched my Archbishop help my wife.

I explained what we hoped to do in America. "Alan, it's taken care of. So see my secretary and she'll organize everything. And by the way, the ticket I'm paying for is for Jenny, not for you. If the Americans don't pay for your ticket, then Jenny goes and you stay." He has a wonderful sense of humor.

Before we left, he said, "You can't just fly directly. It's a long flight and you'll need some rest. I'll tell my secretary to organize a couple of nights for you in Washington, and I'll pay for it." I just looked at him, speechless.

What happened to us during that time was much more important than the airfare to the States. Before we left, he took us into his private chapel and prayed for us, for our journey and for our healing. We felt truly blessed.

Jenny

Over the previous month everything I did required assistance. I had to be helped getting in and out of bed, with dressing, with everything. That Wednesday night after I took my painkillers, I prayed, "Lord, I've really been pushing you about this problem, and I haven't accepted it. If this is the cup that I have to drink from for the rest of my life, I now accept that. I'll have to find a way to live with this, but I'm giving it all back to You. And if there is healing, I give that to You too and thank You for that." Eventually I fell asleep.

On Thursday I was in a lot of pain, so I just rested. Early Friday morning, I needed to go to the toilet. Usually I asked Alan to help me out of bed. But without thinking I got up and started down the hallway by myself. Halfway there I realized that I was walking unaided. I screamed for Alan. He came running, thinking I was hurt. "I don't have any pain," I cried. He just stared at me, so I repeated, "I don't have any pain, and I walked here by myself." It was unbelievable! We both started crying and laughing at the same time.

That day I was afraid to do anything because I thought the pain would come back. But as time passed, I realized I had been healed. In Washington we were able to walk everywhere. I felt so wonderful that Alan had a tough time keeping up with me. And I didn't have to take my medication.

Later when Archbishop Tutu became ill, I wrote to him thanking him for his help and reminding him that God really does heal. Certainly Archbishop Tutu was an instrument for God. He helped me accept my situation and then give it back to God. Once when I told him that, he said, "What did I do? I didn't do anything. It was God."

We are all wounded people, traumatized, all of us, by the evil of apartheid. We all need healing, and we, the Church of God, must pour balm on the wounds inflicted by this evil system. Let us be channels of love, of peace, of justice, of reconciliation.

– Archbishop Desmond Tutu

Alan and Jenny's story illustrates the depth of oppression that people can experience under the most horrendous situations and yet not necessarily lose their soul or their dignity. Often scorned and treated as unworthy third-class citizens, Alan and Jenny suffered rejection, degradation and humiliation. Fortunately there were thoughtful people, including caring whites, who offered them support. And they had a strong and resilient love that fortified them through the darkest times.

Perhaps the most important ingredient of Alan and Jenny's recipe for healing was their unshakeable faith. They trusted that God would eventually reveal the meaning of their anguish and the direction for their service. A deep faith in the Divine can help us get through some of the most troublesome times and provide us with a sense of comfort that whatever happens will ultimately have a useful purpose and a worthy outcome.

Archbishop Desmond Tutu also played an important role in Alan and Jenny's healing. He cared for them like a gentle shepherd and wise mentor — something many of us yearn to have — and to be. He also encouraged them to minister to him in his needs — one of the surprising and transforming gifts of reciprocal healing.

ANNA

Tower of Understanding

*Certainly we victims were deeply harmed.
But I wonder how those who committed the hideous crimes
could possibly live on as though nothing had happened.
I no longer feel hatred toward them, but rather a kind of compassion.*
— Anna

I felt drawn to Anna the minute I saw her white, braided hair lit by a beam of sun from the skylight in the dining room of St. Gerold's Monastery in Austria. Susanne Wey, my friend from Zurich, and I were visiting spiritual and healing shrines throughout Switzerland. Earlier that morning we had driven to St. Gerold's. In the simple chapel, we paused to admire the famous Black Madonna who seemed to gaze tenderly at us from her perch on the wall.

We were delighted when the monks invited us to have lunch with the guests. As we entered the plant-filled dining room, I walked directly toward the woman who had caught my attention. Up close, Anna's sad but gentle smile reminded me of the Madonna's.

As though we had been friends in an earlier time, we began exchanging thoughts about our life journeys. Anna told me she was a Jew; she and her family had been prisoners in a Nazi concentration camp in Germany. After lunch we walked to her room where she continued unfolding her disturbing story.[1] Through the windows I could see the regal Austrian Alps coated with a fresh layer of snow. They provided a dramatic contrast to Anna's dark tale.

Anna

I was born in Hungary a few months before the start of the First World War. My mother's parents were of German origin and the language of their home was German. Her father, my grandfather, was a very pious and scholarly Jew, well respected in his community. My family decided I would learn a trade that would enable me to find a job anywhere, so I was enrolled in a well-known school for dressmakers in Vienna in 1932. Unfortunately, I hated to sew.

In the troubled years before the Second World War, the Nazis came to power in Germany, and we heard terrible rumors about them. At the time I hardly cared because I had discovered dancing and was hooked on it. My greatest joy in life was taking dance lessons. While dancing, I could forget my hated profession.

Life moved on without our recognizing the signs of imminent disaster. Then on March 13, 1938, our destiny came crashing down on us. I had been visiting friends in town, and as I started to go home, the Germans marched in. The people of Vienna seemed jubilant. They screamed for joy as they hung like clusters of grapes from the lampposts on the Ringstrasse. My family crawled into our apartment immobilized with fear and despair,

---

[1] Anna has written a book about her life: Kopp, Anna. *Eine Heimat für die Seele: Vergeben–Nicht Vergessen.* Hameln: Niemeyer, 1995. Some information for this chapter has been taken from Anna's book with her permission. Translations by Susanne Wey.

realizing we were the only family in danger in our apartment building. Immediately our neighbors not only isolated us but asked us to understand their behavior.

One night I had a date with a young man whom I had recently met. He wanted to show me his new motorbike, so I got on the back seat and we took off. Soon I was enjoying myself and wishing we could drive on like that forever, leaving my troubles behind. Our ride ended at the Kahlenberg, where we sat in a coffee shop directly under the picture of Hitler, "the Führer." Paralyzed with fear, I finally admitted to him my situation. He turned pale as he realized his danger by being in my company. To his credit, he drove me to a streetcar that I took home. I never heard of him again.

Through the years we lived in Vienna, we had kept our Hungarian passports. Now it was advantageous to be foreigners and to have some special protections. The streets of Vienna were full of SS men who could take you away if you could not identify yourself as an Aryan or a foreigner.

Almost everyone started looking for ways to emigrate. People crowded in front of embassies all day long trying to get visas. An American visa was the most favored and most difficult to obtain. There were only a few green cards available, and you had to know someone who would provide you a guarantee. We had no friends or relatives abroad and no means to buy visas.

One of our aunts came to see us, and she begged us to go back with her to Czechoslovakia, where she thought we would be safer. After all, it was unthinkable that something similar could happen there. Although we yearned to join the family, we turned her invitation down.

Not long after that, we learned how wise it had been not to go there. In 1939 Hitler occupied the Czech Republic and made it part of Germany. The ethnic cleansing began, and Jewish citizens were forced to leave their homes. One of my uncles, a doctor, was immediately taken away. My mother's youngest brother and his family spent several years trying to hide from the Gestapo in the forests. Some kind and generous farmers hid the family and gave them food during the cold winter months. Sometimes they lived only on berries and mushrooms. One of my young cousins once spent weeks hiding inside a cupboard.

Later that year we left Vienna and moved to Budapest where I worked as an assistant to a tailor. Emil, a young lawyer who had shown an interest in marrying me, had received a visa to the States because he was the nephew of a judge there. He wrote and invited me to join him.

In September 1939, we heard on the radio that the Second World War had begun. Just as in Vienna, people were afraid and wanted to get away. With documents from Emil, I went to the American Embassy to apply for a visa. I was told the chances were slim, as the quota for Hungary was very low. The Embassy sent me an official confirmation letter stating that I had applied for a visa. I kept that paper, not knowing how important it would eventually become.

In 1944 the Germans occupied Hungary, and suddenly Nazi signs were everywhere. It had been perfectly planned and organized. As Jews, we felt trapped without any escape route, a horrible shock. We had to be extremely careful since we didn't know who might be a Nazi agent. Many of the concierges in apartment buildings were party members who provided the party information about the tenants' heritage. They controlled with diligence our every move.

Every day brought new rules and orders that both burdened and threatened our lives. If you could not show proof of having four Aryan grandparents, you could be persecuted. Being a member of a Christian church was not adequate.

As non-Aryans, we had to wear the yellow star everywhere. Our apartments were marked, bringing complete and instant isolation. We were also permanently registered and under observation. Anyone who addressed a star-wearer in the street or visited with one could be registered too. We didn't expect people to risk their lives by speaking to us. Families and friends were ripped apart, and we felt like lepers.

After a curfew was set, we were only allowed to leave the house for a few hours each day and were forbidden to use the streetcars. Even shopping became dangerous. Groceries were scarce, and we had to stand in endless lines in front of stores. Often we had to leave the line in order to get home before the curfew. The death penalty was set for anyone who did not respect the rules. Although we had no precise information, we heard about the concentration camps and knew we could be sent there for any violation.

Then the bombing began. Budapest had no shelters, so we took refuge in the basement of our building. It was depressing to wait for hours, often through the entire night, in damp, dark rooms while our neighbors stared at us and we listened to the falling bombs. In many ways we were more relaxed than our neighbors because we had nothing to lose. We knew, if we survived the bombings, we would be threatened by more malice. At times we wished a bomb would hit us and end our suffering.

One day the concierge told us that the next day my sister and I were to report to a sports stadium and to bring everything we needed with us. We knew what this meant. The older people were allowed to stay in the apartment and would be sent later to the ghetto. Our mother was spared for the time being.

The following day my sister and I went to the stadium with a few of our papers, some food and the clothes we were wearing. The stadium was packed with people. We felt certain we would be sent to a concentration camp in Germany. We spent several days and nights there, sleeping outside in the cold with almost no food or water.

Then we heard that all foreigners were to identify themselves. Although Hungarians, we decided to claim we were Americans, using the letter from the U.S. Embassy that confirmed my application for a visa. It was risky, but the letter was in English and had big official stamps on it. After checking our papers extensively, a man decided we should go back to town with other foreigners. Later we heard he was from the Swiss consulate; he was trying to save whomever he could.

The soldiers took us to a school. We felt relieved since we thought we would never return. Although only a short delay, each day was a bonus and might bring a change in our luck. A few days later when the man from the Swiss consulate came to check on our group, we told him we were worried about our mother. He promised to see what could be done.

Mother arrived the next day with a few of her things, and we believed we were no longer in danger. Unfortunately we didn't know that by coming there she missed the chance to survive in the ghetto as some of her peers did.

Mother brought several colorful wool balls with her, so I designed and knitted the most beautiful sweater I had ever made. My fears, hopes and dreams were in it. Sometimes I reflect on the sweater's whereabouts or if the person wearing it had any idea how it had been created.

A Hungarian professor of medicine, his wife and two daughters were in our group. He found a corner in the attic where he put his record player, and each night we listened to his records of Beethoven's Sixth Symphony, the "Pastorale." This music became so closely connected with our situation that I cannot listen to it today without getting upset.

During the four weeks in the schoolhouse, we became accustomed to living in tight quarters with little to eat. Rumors that the war was ending and the German troops were drawing back nurtured our optimism. So we vacillated between hope and despair, but we didn't believe there was a real threat to us.

Our rude awakening came like lightning. One day we were assembled in the school's courtyard where a "doctor" checked each person briefly and asked our ages. My sister and I were happy to be put into the same group as our mother. Surrounded by young Nazi troops, we were marched out of town. As we walked, prisoners and prostitutes joined us.

It was a long and miserable trek to the concentration camp, and each day the situation got worse. As we walked along, we were mocked by the criminals and prostitutes, who felt superior to us. Because they were Aryans, our guards did not bother them much. We were extremely hungry and thirsty and soon lost our energy and stamina. As our clothes got wet and soggy, they became heavy to drag along on our weak bodies. Our shoes slowly disintegrated, making every step very painful. I can't remember how we dealt with our hygiene problems or relieved ourselves. Perhaps these problems didn't exist since we barely ate or drank.

Those who could not walk fast enough were shot. Daily our numbers decreased. My sister and I put Mother between us and dragged her along. I had always felt emotionally neglected by my mother, and our relationship was strained. But on this dreadful walk, I felt tremendous sadness that her life was ending under such awful circumstances. It felt like an iron ring that had been binding my heart burst, and I was able to hug her and console her.

The nights were horrible. Often we slept outside, sometimes in freezing cold rain. Sometimes we were shoved into huge brick-baking kilns, with the door locked behind us. Inside it was absolutely pitch black, and we held on to each other to keep from getting lost. Total panic came over us. It's amazing we survived without losing our minds.

The culmination of horrors was the night the guards told the female prisoners to stand in a line with the male criminals lined up opposite us. Some women were chosen as the victims, and the men were forced to rape them while the guards watched and laughed. My sister was chosen, and a man who looked like a beast grabbed her and brutally raped her right in front of our mother and me. It was cruel and barbaric.

As we were driven through Hungary and Slovakia to the German border, we became completely exhausted, and our numbers continued to dwindle. When we thought we couldn't walk a step further, we reached a German city. Ironically, I thought we would be safe there. After all, Germany was a nation of culture, the country of my admired Goethe. Surely the Germans would end the evil spell of the guards. As we walked past a group of elegant SS officers, I heard one of them call us "lousy, filthy Jews."

That night as we were being locked in an old school building, a soldier asked about my profession. When I told him I was a seamstress, he asked if I knew how to sew men's shirts. I said "yes" even though I didn't have a clue how to do it. I was clinging to the smallest shred of hope. He told me I would start work in the morning.

A short time later the soldier motioned me to come to the door. I was shocked when he handed me an unexpected treasure, a bottle of milk. I was so hungry and thirsty that I couldn't resist drinking a few sips on the way to my mother and sister. As I tried to hand them the bottle, my hands were shaking so badly that I dropped it. It shattered as it hit the stone floor. I was devastated because they didn't get one drop of the precious milk.

That night I couldn't sleep as I tried to figure out how to cut out a man's shirt. But early in the morning we were taken to a cargo train and shoved into cattle cars. Because there was no room, we had to stand or sit on the floor. The guards dumped some moldy bread into our car and slammed the door shut. We heard them secure the doors with iron bars.

Now we were certain we were on our way to a concentration camp. Strangely enough we were quite calm and composed. Probably we lacked the energy to feel anxiety — a strange blessing.

As the train moved along, we could barely determine if it was day or night. Inside the car it was very dark, and only a small amount of light filtered in through the cracks in the walls. We had no idea where we were going. We crouched on the floor pressed tightly together with no room to stretch. The train traveled for a long time; then it stood still for many hours.

At one point, I had a strange but wonderful experience as if I had died and left my body. It felt like I was floating, and I had a feeling of wellbeing. This might have lasted for only a few seconds, but I tried to hang on to that impression as it gave me hope and new strength.

Finally the doors were opened, and we were ordered off the train. Then we realized that many of the people who had entered the car with us had died during the trip. Because the space inside the car was too tight for anyone to fall over, we had not even noticed that someone sitting right next to us was dead.

It was totally dark as we got off the train and were marched through the streets of some unknown place. It was like a ghost town, not a single person in sight and all the window shutters closed. I made out the silhouette of a church in the dark and felt consoled that here lived people who went to church and knew the Christian commandments. They could not possibly harm us.

Eventually we walked through the gate of Ravensbruck concentration camp. Some young girls appeared, took all our belongings and thoroughly inspected them. In my bag was the beautiful sweater I had knitted and Goethe's *Lebensweisheiten* (*Wisdom of Life*). One of the girls looked at me in disbelief. "Are *you* reading Goethe?" she asked. I wondered what they had heard about us that they were surprised I was reading Goethe. Had someone told them we were animals and not worthy to live?

When we were registered, we stuck with our claim to be American citizens. Then we had to remove our clothes and go naked to a room with showers. I had heard stories about showers that poured out gas. But I had pushed this out of my mind as impossible. As I stood under the shower, I realized it could be real. However, the thought did not upset me.

But out of the showerhead came water, not gas. As we left the showers, we were given some ragged clothes, which I never once changed in all the time I spent at Ravensbruck. We were also given the yellow star, a number and a mess tin bowl. Then we were sent to "the block." In the blocks we slept in racks of raw wood stacked on top of each other. Three people slept together in each rack like sardines in a can. There were no covers and no pillows. We quickly learned to use our mess tins as our pillows so they wouldn't be stolen.

Our daily life in Ravensbruck began each morning while it was still dark. The door was ripped open, and a woman with a piercing voice shouted awful insults at us and called us to inspection. This should have gone quickly, as we had no clothes to put on and no way to wash ourselves. But it seemed to go on for hours. We were told that anyone who could not stand upright during inspection would be sent to the "furnace." We knew this was not an empty threat as we often breathed in the putrid-smelling smoke in the air.

Some of our guards and torturers were prisoners from Poland, France and Belgium who were not Jews. In our eyes they seemed to have a wonderful life. While we stood outside for inspection in all kinds of foul weather, they took turns guarding us and warming themselves at a wood stove in the guard office. Likely the price for their comfort was their vicious behavior towards us.

After inspection we were given a piece of bread and some unidentifiable dark liquid that was poured into our tins, which was supposed to last us the entire day. We quickly learned it was best to eat everything right away, because if we tried to save something for later it would probably be stolen. After eating, we were counted and given heavy shovels, which were nearly impossible for us to carry in our condition. Then we were marched to our work area where we shoveled huge hills of sand from one place to another — a meaningless activity.

Outside the blocks we were guarded by female soldiers, who seemed less cruel than the block guards. Once as I was working, one of the soldiers talked to me as if I was a human being. I felt truly grateful.

At the end of the day the whole routine was repeated. We were marched back to the block where we stood for another long inspection before being given something to eat. Almost every evening we received the same thing, a big spoonful of sour vegetables. Sometimes the guards hit us with their heavy serving spoons. If we had no tin, we got nothing.

The days passed endlessly with the same monotonous rhythm. We had no idea what month or day of the week it was. Many did not survive. Each morning we heard the command to bring out the dead in a wheelbarrow. Everyone was afraid of the dreaded diarrhea, which may have been caused by typhoid from the polluted water. In spite of this, sometimes we couldn't resist drinking from the dirty water pipe because of our endless thirst.

The last winter of the war was extremely harsh, so only one guard would watch over us as we waited in the cold. Sometimes as we stood up to our knees in snow, we talked quietly with each other even though it was strictly forbidden. We never said one word about our present situation, as if by not acknowledging it we could make it unreal. And we never spoke about the future; it was better to repress thoughts about it since we didn't know if there would be one. This masterly feat of our minds was born out of sheer desperation. Occasionally we talked about ways to prepare food — not about simple dishes, but elaborate, elegant meals. I learned much about cooking.

It was almost impossible for my mother to bear the hard work, so I devised a rather dangerous plan. One evening I left our group at the gate and walked to the senior guard's office. It seemed a surreal dream as I stood in front of her explaining that the three of us were skilled seamstresses and could do more beneficial work for them. To my surprise, she told us to report to the sewing commander the next morning.

The next day we began sewing underpants for the army. The work was easy for us, and we were out of the cold. Also it seemed less difficult to do something that felt more "meaningful" than shoveling sand. For a short period of time we were as happy as we could be under the circumstances.

All went well until my mother became ill, probably from typhoid. She had to go to the *revier*, a shed for the sick. Our mother was on the bed near the window, so we could wave to her as we went to and from work. A few days later, the woman in the next bed motioned to us that our mother had died. We left our group to see her. She had just died, and her face had a peaceful expression as if she had seen something wonderful. We felt she had been redeemed and were grateful her difficulties had come to an end. Watching her suffer and not being able to help her had caused us a great deal of pain.

A new blow occurred a few weeks later. At the sewing workshop we were carefully examined for lice. Of course, everybody had them, not only on hairy parts of our bodies, but also on our skin and in our filthy clothes. Because our senses were so numb, we barely had any reaction to the itching. My sister was found infected with lice, and immediately we were sent back to shoveling sand.

We began to hear the bomb alarms more frequently. The guards seemed nervous and were crueler to us. But that had no real connection to our daily life. We only hoped for a swift end to the war.

One morning I woke up with a very high fever and could barely get out of bed, so I reported sick and was sent to the *revier*. There were no doctors to take care of us, and the only advantage was that I could rest. All day long I heard the moaning of the sick and their desperate calls for the bedpan. As my mother once had done, I lay close to the window and saw my sister as she passed on her way to work.

One day she came to the window very upset. "You must leave here immediately," she cried. "The *revier* will be cleared out tonight." We knew what this meant. It was a way of making room for more ill people. We would hear a lot of screaming and the next day would smell the intolerable smoke from the incinerators. I hesitated, not wanting to leave my bed, but with great effort my sister pulled me through the window and dragged me to our block.

Fortunately the guards did not notice us, and I fit in with everyone else because I was wearing the same rags we wore day and night, healthy or sick. Without doubt my sister saved my life; that night the *revier* was emptied.

As the fighting got closer to our camp, there were many changes: Discipline was lacking, there was no work and we had almost no food.

Each day we prayed for the end of the war. It was springtime, and although the landscape was almost barren, the warming light of the sun brought us hope.

As the Allies drew closer, the commanders of the camp seemed more nervous. They began to hand out Red Cross packages from America to the foreign prisoners. Then it happened: The camp commander called out the names of my sister and me. "This is it. Now it's our turn," we thought. But instead of being marched to the incinerators, we were asked if we were Americans. When we answered "yes," we were given a care package from the Red Cross. Somehow we made it back to our block and opened the box containing fantastic treasures: chocolate, sardines, raisins, dried milk powder.

Unfortunately, these wonderful goodies proved to be harmful for us. Although we shared everything with our block friends, we ate too much for our starving stomachs to handle. We gulped down most of the chocolate and sardines and mixed the milk powder with contaminated water. I only got an upset stomach, but my sister became violently ill and went to the *revier.* I tried to sneak in to see her every day, but it was getting more dangerous to risk discovery by the SS soldiers who guarded the place with dogs.

One day a woman prisoner came to our block and told me that there were busses outside to take all foreign prisoners to Sweden and I should go immediately to the gate. I told her I had to go to the *revier* to get my sister. "That isn't necessary," she insisted. "The sick have already been taken away in ambulances, and your sister was with them."

In spite of my uneasy feeling, I didn't listen to my inner voice telling me to look for my sister. Fearing I might not make it to the busses on time or that someone might stop me from leaving the camp, I rushed with my heart pounding to the gate. There stood the famous busses of Count Folke Bernadotte, the president of the Swedish Red Cross, to take away the foreign prisoners from the German camps.

For the last time we "foreigners" stood for inspection as the camp commander instructed us not to take too many bad memories with us. Strangely his words sounded only somber and pathetic to me. Perhaps he realized what he had done and that he would be held responsible not only by the world's judges, but by his own conscience.

Finally our names were called. When the commander read my sister's name, he added: "Already deceased." I started to protest, but the same woman who was standing beside me assured me: "It's a mistake. I know your sister is already on her way to Sweden. Hurry, get on the bus." So I did.

When we arrived in Denmark, I inquired about those who were ill, but my sister was not among them. I was able to console myself that perhaps she had gone by another transport. We traveled on to Sweden. After several days as a refugee, I was interviewed by a Swiss ambassador. I begged him to search for the whereabouts of my sister. Much later I learned my sister had lived in the camp until the Russians freed it in 1945. She died later that summer in a hospital. Perhaps someone else had been taken away from the camp in her place.

I will always regret not personally checking to see if my sister had been taken away by ambulance. I believe it was the greatest sin in my life. I continue to feel shame and sorrow about that.

In the years that followed my release, I developed numerous health problems. The connection from my throat to my stomach became very tight, making it difficult for me to swallow. I went through unpleasant surgeries and treatments that were not successful. My tightness was caused by emotional problems that could not be cured with a knife or medications. I had likely "swallowed too much" in life. Over time I have accepted these disorders and have learned to live with them.

Several years ago my children, who are grown adults, surprised me with a special gift. On a voucher was written "A weekend in a monastery." It was a Catholic monastery not far from Hamburg that had various lectures and courses. Initially I was afraid to go. I might be driven away in disgrace if they learned I was not a Catholic. With a closed heart I went.

A small, interesting group of people had gathered by the time a young monk entered the room. He confessed that we were his first group and he was a little nervous. He was very kind, and I found myself relaxing in the group. At the end of the day, the monk told me that as he looked at the people gathered there, he sensed that I needed care and healing.

That experience launched a whole new life for me. I returned frequently to the monastery for lectures and for healing conversations with the young monk. He told me he often prayed that my soul would find a home, which is exactly what I needed. Through his recommendation, I eventually visited St. Gerold's Monastery, a place where the monks believe their calling is to provide a "home" for people who are in need.

Soon I was going regularly to St. Gerold's where I was always received in an open, loving manner. No one tried to convert or influence me in any way. It was there that I was encouraged to tell my story. I was told that it was important for me to review and write about my life and that time in history, that it should never be forgotten, that few witnesses are still surviving.

When I began writing my story, I reflected back on the Holocaust and that dreadful time in history. The horrendous atrocities that occurred could not have happened without the help of the wider world. Most governments were well acquainted with the ideas and work of the Nazis. It was not a secret. Yet they stood by and watched without taking action, allowing millions of people to be killed. Countries could have kept their borders open for refugees and welcomed some of them. Many bitter fights took place over escape documents, and people were often cheated out of their last pennies for worthless visas. The institutional church also failed by remaining silent and pretending not to see. The whole world should be judged in this matter.

Unfortunately, humankind has not learned much from this experience. Daily, in many places of the world, the same things are happening.

As time goes by and I feel more healed, I am able to think about the people who tortured and guarded us. I often wonder how they dealt with their roles during that atrocious period. Were they able to go home after work and behave as if they were tired from some kind of honest work? Did they reflect on what they were doing? Were they able to play happily with their children, romance their wives or husbands, or walk the dog after they had heartlessly killed and cruelly hurt uncounted numbers of people in inhuman ways? Did they go to church and pray the Lord's Prayer? Or did they feel no guilt because they thought they had merely extinguished unworthy lives?

As a victim it's important for me to try to understand but not allow myself to fall into despair. I will always feel deep pain — not only for those of us who were the victims, but also for the perpetrators. Certainly we victims were deeply harmed. But I wonder how those who committed the hideous crimes could possibly live on as though nothing happened. In my heart I believe that no normal human being is capable of doing such things. There is no way that I would have wanted to change positions with my torturers. Therefore, I no longer feel hatred toward them, but rather a kind of pity and compassion.

If you want to see the brave, look at those who can forgive.
If you want to see the heroic, look at those who can love in
return for hatred.

— Bhagavad-Gita

As I listened to Anna, I realized how important it was for her to tell her story — that each telling served as another piece of her healing process. It enabled her to bring her shame and anguish out of the dark corners of her mind where they had the potential to fester and do harm.

For Anna and those of us who have experienced deep traumas, the healing process will likely be a lifelong challenge. We too can use storytelling as a way of coming to terms with our adversities and pain. By reviewing our story, we can face our fears and reconnect with buried feelings. Wounds of misery and suffering can lose their lethal power if they are brought into the open within a meaningful and healing context.

As Anna talked, I found myself thinking about my grandparents, who came from Germany and could have qualified as "Aryan." When I was growing up on a farm in Nebraska during the Second World War, cattle were sometimes killed and barns burned on the property of people of German descent. My grandmother was not allowed to speak German with me, and my mother instructed me never to admit our family had come from Germany. I was just an American. In a world of refugees and immigrants, there are many people whose roots were in countries that have been so-called "enemies" — Russians, Japanese, Afghanis, Iranians, Vietnamese, Germans. We too need healing from our "shame."

Most people who have lived through what Anna has experienced would be filled with bitterness and a desire for revenge. In a landscape filled with racism and hatred, Anna has chosen to view her predators with forgiveness, compassion and understanding, thus sowing a tiny seed of hope in the world.

TOM

Tower of Transformation

When I was first locked up, I started asking where were all those things I had believed in? I'd gone down about as far as I could go, almost over the edge. Fortunately through those dark days, I always had support. – Tom

I first learned about Tom from a newspaper article: "Ex-convict speaks to students and community groups about making wise choices regarding drinking and driving." Tom had been a family man and a very successful businessman before the fateful night when he drove his BMW while under the influence of alcohol. A passenger was killed in that car, and his life changed dramatically after he was convicted of manslaughter. The reporter pointed out that even if Tom "could count the number of lives he saves, he wouldn't count them as atonement for the one life he ended."

It seemed Tom was doing something rare in our culture: accepting responsibility for what had happened and trying to make amends. He looked like a worthy candidate for a book on healing.

I interviewed Tom in his stark living room sitting on folding chairs beside a small card table. As Tom talked, it struck me that this man had been the "American success story." His parents were upright, middle-class Irish Catholics who valued a good education for their children. Tom did well in school, was never in trouble, had a lovely family, and made bundles of money. One night of bad choices erased that picture. Now Tom was starting over — folding chairs and all.

Tom's story could be almost anyone's story — yours or mine.

Tom

On the morning of February 17, 1994, everything seemed to be going great in my life. My family's business was very successful, and I had lots of control and power. I was doing long hours, running hard, and felt bigger than life. I wore Armani suits and Gucci shoes and drove a BMW. I had no idea everything in my world would abruptly change that night and all my good choices and hard work would disappear.

It was a typical day: I got up, drank a cup of coffee, put on one of my expensive suits and took off in my fancy car. For five hours I met with my corporate attorneys working on a deal for the business. After the meeting, I headed to a trade show. I had not eaten breakfast or lunch. It was just go, go, go.

After the show, I had a drink at the cocktail hour — standard stuff with trade shows and customers. It was already eight o'clock and I was tired. The next day I had to be in Boston for a meeting, but I didn't want to drive that night. I called an old friend, and we met at a local restaurant where I had a beer and a half and a cup of coffee. Then we hung out at my friend's house and I had a couple more beers. About 11 o'clock I decided it was time to go to my hotel.

On the way I thought, "I hate hotels. I don't want to go there yet." I had been spending too many nights on the road. Every hotel, whether it was the Ritz or the Marriott or Motel 6, seemed the same: a strange bed, a television, and a clicker — click, click, click. I'd usually get to sleep after one in the morning. So I decided to stop for one more drink. At the bar I had a cocktail and started to leave. Three young men were sitting at the bar, and we started talking and joking around. They bought me a round and I bought them one — something like that. The memories are not clear. Obviously I was pretty high. According to the police report, I asked if someone could get me a taxi or drive me across town to my hotel.

The next thing I remember was waking up in the hospital on a gurney looking up at bright lights and white walls. I couldn't figure out where the hell I was. A state trooper was looking down at me. "What happened?" I asked. "You crashed your car at 100 mph into the back of a city snowplow and killed your passenger," he answered. "I need to know his name." I didn't believe him. I'm one of the safest drivers I know. I didn't have a single speeding ticket on my record, never had an accident in my life and never had a problem with alcohol. I couldn't remember having a passenger in my car, and I certainly didn't know his name. That was the truth.

I was covered with blood — some mine, but most from the young man who had died in my car. He had died horribly and instantly. The car was totally destroyed. According to the report of the accident, I was driving my car down an entrance ramp to the highway about 12:15 A.M. As I came onto the highway, I tried to pass a snowplow on the left side. Obviously I misjudged my speed and hit the front right of the car. I was seat-belted; my passenger wasn't. There was an airbag on my side of the car but none on the passenger side. So I had only minor injuries: a broken right hand, a bunch of cuts, and a bandaged head. He died.

They tested my blood for alcohol content, and I was arrested and booked. I was immediately thrown into a cell in the local jail with three teenage boys, who were in for possession of heroin. When I saw them, I thought, "Boy, are they in trouble!" I had no real understanding of my situation, where I was, or what was going on. I was totally in shock. The young guys were arraigned first. One of the kids came back to the cell and said, "Did you hear there's a guy in here who crashed his car over 100 miles an hour and killed somebody? Boy, is he screwed!" That's when it hit me that I was in big trouble.

The police said I was awake the whole time at the scene of the accident and that I told the ambulance people, "Don't worry about me. Take care of him first." Of course, he was already dead. But I don't remember that. It's all fuzzy to me; I have no memory of the accident or even getting into my car. Later in counseling I was told when you have a major blow to the head and are in shock, you can lose short-term memory. It has not come back to me. I have only one flashing glimpse of pulling around to the left of what I thought was a construction truck. But it wasn't a truck; it was a snowplow.

I was arraigned around ten the next morning, and bail was set at $25,000. I didn't know what to do, so I called my mom and dad who were in Europe at the Olympics. I had no idea what time it was in Europe. I heard my dad's sleepy voice on the phone: "Is everything okay, Tom?" "No, dad, I killed somebody in my car. I need you." They packed up immediately and got the first flight back to the United States to try to save their hotshot son. My next phone call was to my wife. "Is everything all right, Tommy?" she asked. "No, I killed a man last night." In the middle of February she packed our little children in the car and drove to New Hampshire to save her hotshot husband. My wife hired an attorney for me, and we went home to Vermont. I felt absolutely worthless.

Those first days were very bad for me. In fact it was a terribly dark time for quite a while. My folks were emotionally supportive, but they didn't know what to do. The whole family was distressed: "What does this mean? What do we do?" None of us had ever had any experience with the law or with anything like this, so we had no response mechanism to deal with it. My kids, who were only three and six, were confused by everything. I just lay in bed completely depressed.

It's difficult for me to think back on that period since there was so much despair and everything was very black. I could function, but I was not in a position to care for myself. I had no idea what to do. Everything felt out of control. And the legal process started coming down the tracks like a freight train.

Initially I was arrested for negligent homicide, but I was indicted for manslaughter. There's a big difference between the two crimes.

Negligent homicide implies that you had no intention. Manslaughter is a greater degree of negligence. The basis for manslaughter: I was aware that I was drunk because I asked people to drive me and asked the manager to get me a cab. Because I was aware of my condition, still chose to drive, and then allowed someone to ride with me made it a greater degree of negligence.

With negligent homicide, I was looking at a sentence of one to three years. With manslaughter I was facing possibly eight to sixteen years. That's a lot! The prosecutor was a very motivated man whose major focus was on alcohol-related fatalities. He was on a crusade. I was a white-collar guy, driving a fancy car and worth a lot of money. I represented another tier that he could send a message to, and I was the message. "It can happen to you too. It doesn't matter if you have money or not, white collar or blue collar." He wanted to change the inaccurate perception that drunk drivers were only blue-collar alcoholics.

In my world, I was brought up to believe that if you're guilty you admit it, you take the heat for it and try to make it right. I approached my trial knowing I was responsible for a young man's death. So I pled guilty to the charge of manslaughter since I was guilty. I wrote the victim's family a letter because I wanted them to know the truth and to hear from me how sorry I was. I didn't make excuses for my behavior. The man who had died in my car that night had a son — the age of my son. Writing the letter was against my lawyer's advice because it implied my guilt. The family didn't respond to my letter, and I don't know if it helped. But through this whole process, I've felt they have been very supportive of me — a miracle in the truest sense of the word. Years later when I started speaking at high schools, the family was often there.

At my sentencing, the courtroom was filled with almost everyone I knew. My family and my attorneys sat on one side. They tried to paint the best picture of me and tell the world what a good guy I was. Meanwhile the assistant attorney general and the victim's family were on the other side. The prosecution painted the worst. I went from being a wonderful super man on one side, which was not the truth, to an evil person on the other, which also wasn't the truth.

When the judge banged her gavel and said, "Mr. Boyle has pled guilty to manslaughter," it really hit me. It didn't matter that many people had spoken on my behalf about what a wonderful guy I was. Mr. Wonderful got sentenced for manslaughter because my passenger, a young man, had been killed. When the sentence was read, it was a very emotional time. I was given an opportunity to speak before I was taken away. I cried when I said that I accepted responsibility for what I had done and I was sorry.

Immediately after that, the guards shackled my hands and feet, and I was brought through the courtroom past everyone I knew. My father-in-law said to me as I left the room: "Tom, you will not be remembered for what you did. You will be remembered for what you do from here on out." I tried to hold on to that. It gave me a thread of hope that might bring some dignity and self-respect back into my life.

Then I was taken to the basement of the courtroom to a cell with bars on everything. My attorneys were really excited: "You didn't get eight to sixteen years! You only got four to eight." Like I had just lucked out and won the lotto. Four to eight years of my life, and I was the lucky guy.

All my material goods were removed — my watch, suit and shoes. I was handcuffed and taken to prison. I went through two sets of gates and chain-link barbwire fences. "So far so good," I thought. "I can manage this. I'm all right." Then I went through a heavy metal door that was slammed and locked behind me. Suddenly everything was gone. Everything I knew and loved and cared about in my world was on the other side of that door. I was terrified.

Prison is not like the movies. It's about misery and loneliness every day. You do what you're told to do: eat, work, sleep, anything. As soon as I was inside, I was given a little green bottle of disinfectant and told to scrub down with it so I wouldn't pollute the other prisoners. While people were walking around going about their business, I was scrubbing in the shower with nothing on. Then I was fingerprinted and given my new prison outfit. And the number 22466 — that's who I was.

At first I was put in a room for about three weeks where the lights were on 24 hours a day. I was really scared. During that time, I was only allowed to go outside in a caged area for one hour. There was nothing to read and nothing to do. Nobody talked to me. I had to scrub cells. I was just serving time. I didn't know when I would get out. Somehow I survived.

Everybody knew my stuff, that I was educated, white-collar, wealthy. They had seen the newspaper article "Millionaire goes to prison." It wasn't a time to break down or to show signs of weakness. My instincts had to be up all the time. It was a constant struggle watching out for everyone — cops and inmates. I didn't know who was a threat. I couldn't be too friendly with the cops or with certain inmates. I asked a lot of questions and tried to figure out the game.

Then I was moved to a locked-down, hot and miserable section of the prison with really tight quarters. The cells were four-by-eight, double-bunked, with a toilet — period. Although I was only in there for a couple of months, it seemed like forever. I ended up living with an Irish guy who allegedly robbed a store. Being Irish myself helped. He put the word out through the prison wire: "This guy's all right. I want you to take care of him."

After a few months, I was moved to a very noisy and threatening unit with open, ten-man cells. People took other people's stuff; there was often loud rap going on until two in the morning. It was a wild scene. I was in a constant mode of thinking how I should present myself. I didn't want to be a lightweight, but at the same time I didn't want to be threatening. Fortunately I was in a cell with guys who had done some time and were fairly well-respected.

After about five months of prison life, I got a good job in the education department teaching classes toward high school diplomacy. The average age of the guys in my classes was about 18 or 19 years. Prior to that I had cleaned toilets and scrubbed floors, so working in education felt like a big deal. Because I was doing something for the other guys, I was generally respected.

Eventually I was moved to "general population," a place for longer-term prisoners who were not in a high level of custody or lockdown. At first I was frightened because I had to mix with so many people. But it turned out to be a good place. I was put in a pod with twenty-four men.

Eighteen of them were doing huge numbers: life, life without, 15 to 30 years. In comparison I was just a short-term guy. The guys I lived with were recognized as the most respected and coolest men in the prison, the ones you didn't mess with. It took me a while before they let me participate in their world. They showed me the ropes, taught me how to get by and were like a family for me. Their acceptance made my time inside much easier. We played cards, cooked pots of spaghetti on weekends and played basketball.

After being in prison for a few months, I was able to have more visits and phone calls. My mother, who is a remarkable woman with a deep faith, sent me a card every day, even if it was just a postcard with "Love, Mom." No matter where she was, she did that. It was unbelievable. Sometimes I tell people: "I was in a dark place, so dark that I couldn't see anything except for a tiny, little light. Through that tiny light, my mother reached down, grabbed me and pulled me up."

The mail, the phone calls and the visits kept me going. Getting visitors and mail meant somebody loved me and I had support. It also had an impact on how I was perceived on the inside. If somebody loved me, I was worthwhile. Often when people go to prison, they aren't loved very much and almost never get mail or visits.

Visits took place in a large room with tables and chairs. It was a fairly decent, open environment — not behind a screen — so I could hug and hold my kids. I usually had several visits a week from my family and business associates. My wife and children came to see me for about an hour and a half every two or three weeks. It wasn't a lot of time to be with my babies. My son, who's very smart in math, figured out that we would end up seeing each other about 25 hours a year, only one day a year.

Still, I realized I was the lucky guy. The man who had been killed in my car was no longer around. In one night everything was taken from him, and his son would never see his dad.

One day I received a letter from my wife. It was double-spaced and block printed on yellow legal paper. My heart sank. We were already separated because I was in prison. The letter stated that the divorce was on its way, and she didn't want to talk about it. Of course, I couldn't talk with her because I could only call collect, and someone on the other end had to accept my call.

When I first went to prison, I knew it was possible that the worst of everything could happen: I might end up divorced, my business could go down and my mother might die. She's had problems with her health. But I tried to keep a tiny ray of hope going.

At the beginning of my time inside, I was totally down on myself: I was a bad father, a bad husband, a bad son, a bad business partner. But when people on the outside continued to love and support me with visits, phone calls, and mail, I started asking myself: "Okay, what's good about me, what's not?" The combination of having love from the outside and developing an identity within the prison helped give me a sense of myself again. It was something I could lean on.

Although some guys were helpful to me, I couldn't ever get too close to them. I lived with one guy who had killed his two ex-wives. Yet in most of the prisoners there was some good and some evil — as in all of us. I had to accept people for what they were and what they had done. I couldn't get judgmental. And who was I to judge? I had taken someone's life. Many of these men who had done some bad things had not taken a life.

Learning not to be judgmental was a good lesson for me, and I began to see people for what they really were. People are not necessarily what they do. Somebody who robbed a bank can be kind, intelligent, a wonderful communicator. Being in prison does not necessarily mean someone is bad. They may have done bad things, but that doesn't mean there isn't some value in them. Of course, there were also uncaring, violent and immoral people with no sense of right and wrong.

About a year into my sentence, I was doing all right. Then one day I was called up to prison security — a place you didn't want to go. Sitting there was the state trooper who had arrested me. I didn't remember him. He had known the victim, so at the sentencing he wanted me to go to prison for life. But since my imprisonment, he started thinking about the kind of life I had lived before the accident and how at the sentencing I took responsibility for what had happened. "Wait a minute," he thought, "that could be me. Tom was the All-American success story: a small town boy who had made all the right choices until that fatal night." He told me he didn't know anyone who had pled guilty to manslaughter after they had been drinking and driving. Because I had done that, I was paying a big price. Maybe something good could come out of this situation. Would I be interested in pursuing some kind of educational program outside prison?

It was a miracle. There were many miracles in the truest sense of the word: I had a job in education, I ended up living with guys who looked after me, the arresting state trooper wanted to help me. I used to think miracles were big things, but now I know they are everyday little things.

Eventually I was sent to minimum security two years earlier than what was usual. Minimum is a lock-down facility outside the walls for those who are on their way out. There, you're allowed to have a little more freedom before you live in halfway houses and have a job in the community. A process of phase-out. There was lots of tension in minimum. People from the general population were put together with those who had been in protective custody, including child molesters and sex offenders. It was an intentional effort by the prison to force people to fail there if they were going to fail. And there were plenty of opportunities to slip up. Lots of guys were put back inside.

For two years I was assigned a job in the commissioner's office working as the office boy for professionals who were intellectually stimulating. Their positive responses toward me helped me feel, "I'm not an evil person. I'm really okay." They trusted me, which was very healing.

When I had one year left, I was asked to speak at a high school. Nobody inside had ever gone outside of prison to speak. The arresting state trooper had talked with the attorney general's office about the idea of my speaking in schools. They were very engaged in this kind of thing, along with Mothers Against Drunk Driving (MADD).

They took me in handcuffs from prison to the school. I prayed to God: "Help me say what I need to say, and let my words be heard by these kids." When I was given the microphone, I spoke for about 45 minutes to more than a thousand high school students.

The kids were so quiet, you could have heard a pin drop. I told them about the decisions I had made the night of the accident and the results of those choices. "Your folks, teachers and friends can guide you and help you, but you have to learn most lessons in life by yourself. The cost of some decisions can be very great. The choices I made got me to where I am. It's important to make good choices." I kept it to the truth, and I didn't try to sell them anything. Young people know when they hear the truth. My speech was just before the high school's prom, and there were no alcohol incidents that night.

That spring I spoke at six or seven schools. In the next school season, the program was connected with the State Police and the Department of Corrections (DOC), and I spoke at seventy some schools around the state.

Soon the program was rolling along and starting to win some awards. Meanwhile, I was still working in the commissioner's office. At that point, the DOC decided to put me on an ankle bracelet and allow me to live outside. Usually someone is only on a bracelet for three months, but I was on it for a year. I knew they were putting a lot of trust in me, and I felt grateful.

Although still a prisoner, I moved by myself with an ankle bracelet into this house. My good friend Bob let me stay here. I had very little money and being able to stay in a nice house rather than in a cheap apartment gave me some dignity. It was a home where my children could visit me.

A machine was set up in the house that took my picture every day. I had to blow into a breath tester each night. If I was outside my allowed range, I had to inform someone where I was. My parole officers stopped by the house several times a week. Meanwhile, I continued doing the talks at high schools, colleges and community events. A year later, I was paroled. The bracelet came off. I knew I didn't dare screw up. I decided to focus primarily on my work and my children, whom I see every other weekend. It was important for me to have something meaningful to do.

How have I changed from this whole experience? I think I'm a much humbler and less judgmental person. I'm more open to people from different ethnic groups and races. I accept people's failings better than I did before. In prison there were guys from all walks of life and backgrounds. Being with them helped me appreciate my upbringing. I never realized how fortunate I was.

Am I better than the other guys in prison? No, I'm not. I am basically a good human being who has made mistakes. I try to do the right thing more often than not and I don't choose to hurt people. I had always been a communicative and happy person, somewhat idealistic. I was worried I might lose that in prison. In some ways, I've become more protective and careful, but I haven't completely lost my trust in people. I'm still open to their good side.

When I was first locked up, I started asking where were all those things I had believed in? I'd gone down about as far as I could go, almost over the edge. I was afraid I would become bitter, cynical and impersonal. I had to take a hard look at myself — something I hadn't done for at least ten years.

Fortunately through those dark days, I always had support. That kept hope alive for me. It reminded me who I really was, where I had come from and what were the basic things I really could lean on — my upbringing, my family, what I was raised to be, what's in my genes and in my soul. And as I searched deeper, I found my beliefs were intact within me. I knew who I really was. I was the person my parents had raised me to be. I could lean on those things that were core to my upbringing; they would always be there.

Does that mean everything is wonderful now and that I don't have problems to grapple with or relationships that are confusing? Of course not! There's a whole host of difficult things. But I no longer push so hard, and I don't need answers to solve everything immediately. I'm taking life much more as it comes. Things that were big deals five years ago now roll off my back.

There's still stress in my life, but it's not soul frightening. The guys in my office will tell you that I pace up and down the hall with a phone in my ear. I still run at a very fast pace and work long hours tapped into the veins of high-tech, E-mail, voice mail and software. I know where that got me before. I don't want to do it the same way again. Right now I want to try to ensure, to the best of my ability, that my family's financial situations are secure.

Looking back, I know prison was a horrible experience for me. It was about misery and loneliness for what felt like forever. I've forgotten some of the worst moments of fear and panic. People can't fully understand the sorrow and tragedy of it unless they've been there. Everybody has had bad experiences in their world. Some people live their whole lives in misery and fear that are as frightening as prison was to me.

My prison experience also provided me an opportunity to realize that I can choose what I want to do with my life. I had never understood that because I had so many commitments to my family, to my wife, to my children, to the business, to a way of living. Those were all noble excuses for why I was doing what I was doing that allowed me to dodge the question about who I was.

So prison was both confining and liberating for me. Even though I had many concerns while I was inside, I had time to think through things and to listen to myself. I became liberated from the image of the person I thought I should be — the successful businessman with the glass house, the BMW, the fancy clothes and all that stuff. Now my life is more about making conscious decisions and choosing wisely what fits into the big picture.

During those four years, I painted a vision of what I want in my life. I no longer want to compromise something that is precious to me. I believe prison has helped me to put on a new set of glasses, a new set of eyes.

Certainly my personal goals have changed. I look forward to having a simpler life; I know what a fast one brings. My long-range plan is to build a simple, rustic cottage in the woods of Vermont where I can be near my children and focus on their health and wellbeing. It will be a shelter from the storm, a place of peace and tranquility. I'd also like to try my hand at being a basketball coach or a theatre director. As I move along in life, I want to be on the right path making good choices.

Sometimes I wonder if things are meant to be or if it's a person's responsibility to make something of what is. I believe it's the second. Perhaps that is the challenge of life. What I choose to do with people and events will define my character and spirit. As they make contact with me along my journey, they will have a positive impact if I am open to them. If I am closed, I won't be able to see or identify them, and they won't fit in.

I don't feel self-righteous about what happened, and I don't like to give advice. I was a guy who liked to party, and I drank. I ran fast and thought I was in control of life. The choices you make could put you in a situation like mine. It's something that can happen to anyone. It doesn't matter if you are old or young, rich or poor, cool or not cool, jock or non-jock. As soon as you have a drink, your ability to make good choices begins to decline. You put yourself into a situation where you are not in control of what you do, and something could happen that might ruin your life.

Certainly I've learned that from my own tragic experience. I wish I hadn't learned this lesson at such an enormous price: the death of a young man. It's hard to get people to understand this, so I try not to say the words, "Don't drink and drive." I just say, "You're smart. I hope you make better choices than I did. Just use your head."

It was a lifer who wrote to us, "Who could ever imagine a man's freedom being found in prison!" Wisdom can seep in despite or because of anxiety and pain.
— Elaine MacInnes

As Tom told his story, I felt riveted to his words. This young man was honest, decent, and dependable — much-needed commodities in our world. Very few of us have the kind of courage it takes not to make excuses for what we have done, to be responsible for our actions, to accept sometimes frightening penalties for our behavior.

Tom's story points out how healing is often a matter of the choices we make. Through his years of prison, Tom chose not to become bitter or angry. Rather he undertook a process of self-assessment, accepted his losses and came to terms with his strengths and weaknesses. In the process, he freed himself from the image of the person he thought he should be. Ultimately Tom realized that although prison was confining, it was also a liberating experience.

There's a lot to glean from Tom's powerful story. Perhaps we can learn to appreciate people for who they are and not for what they do. Every day each of us can choose to allow the prisons of our lives to restrict us, or we can become liberated from them. We can also choose to walk away from difficult situations, avoid responsibilities and commitments, be a little dishonest. Or we can meet the challenges to be honest and upright and perhaps help ourselves and others to heal — as Tom did.

Faithe and Jud
Towers of Optimism

People tell me that because I project a positive outlook, they are more inclined to offer help. I doubt I would have hooked up with so many people if it weren't for this "hiccup" of MS in my life. — Faithe

What has happened is that we have become closer than we ever would have been if Faithe had not come down with MS. It's a rather bizarre silver lining! — Jud

Faithe is a stunning, intelligent woman with irresistible blue eyes that seem to penetrate your soul. Whenever she smiles at you, it's like fog lifting on a gray London day. I first met Faithe and her husband Jud over 25 years ago when we lived in a revitalized neighborhood in Brooklyn, New York. We shared a number of things in common: We came from the Midwest, we attended a small church in the community, and we had lovingly undertaken the arduous task of renovating 100-year-old brownstone city houses with backyard gardens. I thought Faithe and Jud had it all together:

a good marriage, smart daughter, healthy bodies and minds, interesting work, artistic qualities, a spectacular home and garden. Yes, everything!

About twenty years ago, Faithe and Jud moved to Barnes, a charming suburban community in London. She was just beginning her new life as a garden designer when she was diagnosed with multiple sclerosis in 1991.

Faithe

The first signs that something might be wrong occurred when I was in my late 30s. Every couple of days I jogged a mile, and my knees began to hurt. But I could still play tennis and jog without too much difficulty. In my 40s I started falling down, which was not natural. Initially when I couldn't keep up with Jud, I thought it might be old age. Now I realize I probably had MS for over 20 years. According to the statistics I should have been dead after 17 years!

Several years before my 1991 diagnosis, my doctor in Iowa — where I always went for my physical checkup during our annual family visits — told me that the stiffness in my legs must be arthritis. But the stiffness did not go away and, as the years passed, my feet and lower legs increasingly felt numb. So I went to an orthopedic surgeon who took x-rays and could find nothing wrong.

Finally, an English friend and physiotherapist commented that she doubted I had arthritis. She suggested I get a proper diagnosis. When I returned to the U.S., I made an appointment with a rheumatologist who examined my hands very carefully. "You don't have arthritis," he said. For the first time, I finally asked, "What do I have then?" His response was: "Walk for me." Then I had to stand still with my eyes closed, and he saw that I was weaving back and forth. So simple. I obviously walked and stood with difficulty. Probably no one really believed I was ill, because my bones were strong, I was very athletic, I looked healthy and I didn't complain.

The upshot of that examination was an MRI scan the following day because the doctor thought I might have a brain tumor. That evening he phoned me the results at my mother's home where I was staying: "The good news is you don't have a brain tumor. But you might have multiple sclerosis. More tests are necessary to find out for sure."

I was truly jolted by the news. I had no idea what it meant to have MS. Jud was due to arrive late that evening from England. I had no idea how he would handle the news. I wondered if he might want to leave me. I certainly wouldn't have blamed him. But he didn't. He was very supportive. He just encouraged me to cry. And cry I did! No holding back! I haven't cried like that since, nor have I felt the need to.

After that I had many follow-up blood tests and a spinal tap, but there was no confirmed diagnosis until we traveled to Cleveland for a family visit and saw a top neurologist there. He knew enough to ask the right questions and was very skilled at breaking the news to me, softening the impact with comforting words, "You don't have to think of this as a death sentence or that you'll necessarily even be in a wheelchair in the future. Many MS sufferers continue to lead full lives, but they must take care not to become exhausted or overstressed. And they must respect their limitations." That suited me.

When I first heard I might have MS, I was totally unprepared. By the time the diagnosis was confirmed, I had had time to contemplate the unthinkable, and I felt much more in control. All the little symptoms I'd dismissed in the past were early signs of MS. I'm glad they didn't worry me then, because I wouldn't have tried so many new things — like enrolling in a garden design course and starting a small design business, or buying a spinet piano and recorders in order to play early music. These things have given me great joy, and I'll return to them when they find a cure for MS.

Perhaps the greatest influence on how I adjusted to the lifestyle changes necessary to handle my new reality was the example of my dad. He was a chemistry professor, a talented golfer, a marvelous gardener, and a loving father during our childhood years. He lived to the age of 94 and was miserable for the last 24 years. He was all too willing to share his malaise with anyone within listening range. I observed the toll his behavior took on my mother during his later years and was determined not to emulate his approach to facing adversity.

Shortly after Jud and I moved to England, I saw a wonderful psychotherapist. He helped me learn how to face problems on my own, to be strong and to feel in charge of my life. A favorite saying of his was: "Shit or get off the pot!" Actually, that's not a bad way to deal with this chronic disease. Do what I can and get on with living my life. That way I don't have to blame anyone if things don't go according to plan. I appreciate what I have and try to build on that.

I've been told that I have a fighting spirit. Growing up with my three brothers, I learned early on that battling with one's fists is a losing proposition. Once I was so angry with my older brother that I chased him to his room, but he slammed the door in my face and escaped. Out of frustration I banged and banged on that door, and I really hurt myself. Right then it occurred to me that there must be a better, more effective way to fight.

Certainly there are many ways to solve most problems. What works for one person won't necessarily work for another. Sometimes I ponder why weeds are so successful. Could it be their adaptability? We can learn much from simple observation.

I have never been angry that I had MS. Why shouldn't I have it? Why should someone else have it instead of me? I decided it would be an opportunity to learn firsthand how disabled people feel. In the past I usually avoided acknowledging their presence. That's why I've been so surprised when people, even strangers, acknowledge my existence.

Over the years many people have helped me deal with my illness. The greatest credit goes to my husband Jud. We're a real team. He takes wonderful care of me without doing too much — a hard line to follow. If a spouse does too much, that can foster dependence. Jud has risen to the many challenges MS has presented. It's difficult to live with this disease, to have to worry about finances and care. He's always thinking of ways to make it possible for me to do things and ways to make everything easier for me.

I couldn't cope successfully with MS without the additional moral support of my friends. I'm fortunate to have an assortment of them who share my various interests. Most of them are busy, but they take time to stay in touch and I know I can count on them. I'd lose some of my independence if I had to be totally reliant on any single person.

We bought a small car with automatic everything, but I hate driving in this crowded city, so if I need to go somewhere I gratefully accept a lift on the condition that I pay for the petrol. If I ever get cured, I will happily junk my car and glory in walking and bussing everywhere, using a "car service" only when necessary.

One of the most effective techniques or therapies for me is the use of Peto exercises. I have twice attended three-week training sessions in Budapest at the Peto Institute. In an impoverished post-war Hungary, Dr. Peto developed special exercises to enable physically disabled children to improve their mobility enough to attend the regular state schools, since special education was beyond the means of the state. His success subsequently led to the establishment of a huge institute in Budapest that added an adult education program geared for stroke victims and people with Parkinson's and MS.

For me, exposure to the dedicated instructors and other disabled participants, who were so positive, was a wonderful tonic in and of itself. There were no wheelchairs at the Institute. The first thing I learned was how to get up if I fell. Their whole philosophy is for you to learn how to do things by yourself: get to the bathroom, dress, balance yourself. Some people refused to try some things, but I decided to try everything, even things that looked impossible. After those sessions, I saw improvement in the way I was able to do things. Before I went to the Institute, one of my neurologists was certain I already had permanent damage, but when I returned it had diminished.

Peto exercises are quite easy to do because no equipment is needed. Largely yoga-based, they are not a cure, but I find they make me feel more in charge of the disease, and they negate the need for other professionals who deal with such things as back pain. The exercises can be done at any time, day or night.

I've lost a great deal of mobility since 1992 because chronic-progressive MS moves on relentlessly, but I certainly would be worse off without my exercises, both physically and mentally. Recently I have had greater difficulty sleeping due to foot spasms and back discomfort. So I get out of bed — sometimes in the middle of the night — breathe properly, and do my exercises. Then I've done something positive, and that alone makes me feel better. I can go back to bed minus aches and pains.

Hopefully the combination of exercises and the new MS drugs will help prolong my ability to get around. For some time using my rolling walker was easier than just using my canes. I can still manage with a cane if I take someone's arm on one side. I've tried to avoid being totally wheelchair-bound, but I need to use it more for trips in public gardens or museums. My new power wheelchair is great for getting around and being more independent, and I am able to accompany Jud when he feels like a stroll.

We try to prepare in advance for concerns about the future rather than wait and make changes later under pressure. For example, we had our bathrooms made "disabled-friendly" (raised toilets, power shower with a fold-down seat, grab rails, non-skid floors and so forth) and installed a stair lift, which has made that arduous nightly climb up the stairs to our bedroom unnecessary. So when I am less able and must use a wheelchair regularly, my environment is ready for that.

When a neighbor recently invited us to a party, I first thought how difficult it would be to attend. But then I realized that's not a very positive way to approach life and is a sure way to be excluded in the future. So we went and enjoyed ourselves.

Over the years I've developed my own "recipe" for staying fit and coping. It has really helped me, and I have learned that I can do almost anything I want or need to do — within reason. By practicing these coping skills I believe I'll be able to deal with things as I get worse. My "recipe":

- **P**at myself on the back. Whenever I have accomplished something difficult — like walking a short distance or not falling down or doing my exercises, I pat myself on the back.
- **B**reak down tasks. I try to adapt different activities to fit my abilities and stamina. Instead of tackling the entire garden for hours at a time, I'll do a small one square yard area instead.
- **E**njoy now. I really want to enjoy the present as much as I can, so I try to deal with future problems and get on with living in the here and now.
- **J**ust do it. By doing what I can do and not expecting someone

else to take care of everything, I stay in charge of my life. It's easy to lose my self-confidence, to think that I shouldn't go along with people since they might not want me there because of my disability. But that would mean I would be less active and more isolated. I have chosen not to go that route. People with physical problems or illnesses should not think of being a burden to someone. It's good for people to deal with the disabled now and then.

- **A**sk for help. In my garden, I do what I can and then ask people to help me. We work together. In that way people don't feel sorry for me, and we can enjoy each other's company. Several people have said how much they appreciate my giving them opportunities to help — a gift.

- **D**on't feel sorry for myself. Every person has some problem to deal with. Sure, I'm sorry my MS won't go away. But If I want people to be empathetic to my situation, I can't just sit around and worry about a condition that I've had to live with for many years. I hate being depressed. So if I start to feel that way, I glance in the mirror, and what I see looks so silly that it makes me laugh. Then I feel better.

- **D**on't give up. I'm learning there are ways that I can adjust to whatever disabilities I have. It may be more difficult, but I can still do things. With bridge, the people come to my home and deal the cards for me. It's good because I can have interaction with my friends. I also still paint — but I can only paint for two hours, and I paint smaller pictures. Instead of going to classes, my friend comes here to paint with me.

- **E**xercise every day.

- **K**now my limits. I'm learning not to push beyond what I can do. For example: Eating is more difficult for me since my right hand no longer functions very well. When we eat in restaurants, we choose ones that aren't too crowded so we can manage with my wheelchair or walker. We go early when there are fewer people, and I order food that is easy to cut and eat.

- **M**ake adjustments to each new situation. Certainly things are getting worse. My walking has become more difficult, so we bought a power wheelchair. Although I can no longer play the piano or the recorder because of my hands, I can enjoy listening to music. My talking and writing are worse, but I still work on the computer a little. When I can't do that, I will dictate to Jud or a friend. As I face each new challenge, I make adjustments.

As the MS progresses, nothing is as easy as it used to be. I know it will be more difficult to feel positive as I become more disabled. So I keep my recipe on the wall where I can read it every day.

It's hard to give useful advice. But I strongly recommend that long before you age or are diagnosed with a serious illness, do those things in life that you enjoy. Don't put them off. Make them happen! Don't pay too much attention to other people's advice about choice of career, or the importance of money, or whatever. Develop many interests, diversify your skills and learn to do new things. You may need them. Life is very short — so get on with it!

The things that have sustained me the most are the things I enjoy: gardening, birds, the natural world, companionship. They have been so valuable to me.

Certainly it can be difficult if people don't have adequate resources and they're chronically ill. Yet I believe everyone can still find some part of life to enjoy. For example: Do you like flowers or candlelight or chocolate pudding? Treat yourself to something. Do you want to be with a friend? Do it. If your friends don't seem interesting, find out what they are really like and look for good qualities or something special in them. You may need to cultivate a few new friends. Just don't give up.

I want to conclude with some thoughts about attitude. In fighting MS one never really wins. The way I have "won" has been by being upbeat and positive. It may seem I'm upbeat all the time, but that doesn't mean I never get down. I just refuse to stay down. I only cry when I'm feeling sorry for myself, so I make a real effort to get out of that mood. I take a deep breath and enumerate all the things I have to be thankful for — and I have a lot. This doesn't exactly make my problems go away, but it makes it easier to cope with them. Then I feel better, and it becomes easier to be cheerful.

You can't just tell someone to be upbeat and positive. It comes from having good role models and from being rewarded for being positive. It's not easy to be that way if your family and friends are negative. But anyone can look at a tree or flower and see beauty — if they want. Not everyone will choose to do that.

Certainly, I'd get terribly bored if I just talked about the hardships of my illness all the time. So I try to redirect questions about my health to how others are doing. I am confident people will feel better if they are less focused on their problems, if they can see some of the good in life and focus outside themselves.

My friends have never abandoned me. Let's face it, people prefer to be around positive people; they make better company. I've been told that because I project a positive outlook, folks are inclined to offer help or meet me more than halfway.

Even though I have the kind of chronic progressive MS that gets worse over time, I don't worry about the end of my life. Hey, I've outlived the predictions, so why not keep going? My exercises and upbeat attitude have helped me a lot over the years, and I still have hope there will be something that can help stop the MS. I just want to live fully whatever time I have left.

Dealing with my MS has been a team effort for both Jud and me. We've pulled together, and we both appreciate each other far more than in our earlier years. We're very aware now of what we have and the things that are especially important in life.

I've learned so much from having MS: like people can be wonderful and incredibly helpful. I'm amazed how many people have been loyal and loving to me. I've found friends, family, and strangers so helpful and kind — an unexpected bonus and a revelation. I doubt I would have hooked up with so many people if it weren't for this "hiccup" in my life. In that way, my MS has almost been a blessing.

Jud

Faithe is a remarkable woman. She has developed the ability to deal with the frustrations, worries and hurts of MS and then put them aside. If she's really having a bad day, she might have a little cry. Of course, that upsets me, but at the same time, I appreciate that she needs to do it. I try not to overreact because I know she's going through a difficult period. But once that's over, she puts it aside, smiles and gets on with life.

When I first found out about Faithe having MS, I didn't know enough about the illness to comprehend all of its ramifications. But as I read more about MS, I found out that it comes in different forms, and I became alert to things to avoid and things to be wary of. Then we just "got on with it." I could see fairly early on that it was possible to maintain our lifestyle more or less as it had been, with minor adjustments. But there clearly were things that we jointly had to do differently and things that only I could do.

We're fortunate to be relatively well-off financially at this stage in our lives. So if we had really needed or wanted to, we could have had live-in help. Instead, we have chosen to keep life pretty much as it was. I've simply taken on many of the tasks that Faithe handled over the years and have started doing them myself. In some respects, it's almost been fun, and it definitely has given me a new perspective on life, a real mission. Certainly it's been a challenge, but I believe I have developed the wherewithal to deal with whatever the future holds.

I was fortunate in being able to take early retirement at 55. I had the gift of those extra years and the opportunity to do a lot of interesting things that were on my wish list. Consequently, finding my options in later life narrowed due to Faithe's limitations has not left me with a sense of having been shortchanged or cheated. Nor do I feel that Faithe owes me anything. But my range of options is more restricted now due to her illness, and I increasingly am tied to her — not joined at the hip — as her situation changes.

Like most couples, we have had our ups and downs during the course of our marriage, and on occasion each of us has weighed the desirability of not being married. Knowing how easily frustrated I can get at times, Faithe assured me early on that she would understand if I decided to leave her. But I couldn't conceive of bailing out on her. In the process of pulling together over Faithe's circumstances during the past few years, we have become closer than I ever could have imagined, surely closer than we would have been if Faithe had not come down with MS. It's a bizarre kind of silver lining! I now know a form of love that I might never have experienced otherwise. It's quite different from that of parents looking after a child they have brought into the world. It's part of an adult love relationship. And I need and want to reciprocate freely with my love and caring for Faithe.

I'm not particularly good at dealing with people who are in really dire straits. It would be difficult for me to pity Faithe or to have to give her constant reassurances. In fact, on more than one occasion she has told me that doing so would be counterproductive and simply make it harder for her to cope. I think many people waste too much time feeling sorry for themselves — and for the other person. It doesn't help solve any problems.

In a way, I've enjoyed the challenge of exploring new ways of doing things and of not treating Faithe like an invalid. We've cycled together for many years, especially on holidays in France. It has provided us with some of our most cherished memories. As Faithe's stamina began to diminish and threaten our hobby, one solution was obvious: We bought a tandem bicycle and resumed our cycle touring for several more good years. Faithe was delighted that she could continue biking. Eventually, this type of touring became too much for both of us, and we came up with the idea of canal boating in France. We invested in a power wheelchair that we load into the car and lift onto the boat.

That's just one example of adapting. There will always be something we can do. It may not be the way we would have done it, but if we use a little creativity and stay flexible, there are alternatives.

Faithe's hands have been affected by the progression of her MS during the last couple of years and are somewhat less dependable now. So I have gotten more involved with meal preparation, and I've found I enjoy it — up to a point. My attitude toward cooking: I don't ever want to deal with a recipe that has more than ten ingredients, nor do I want to spend more than one hour in the kitchen. We're fortunate that we can afford to eat out once or twice a week, though my home cooking is not bad.

Since I was already doing the shopping, the whole process has just become more integrated. I now view the shopping, cooking and washing up as another challenge: how to streamline and simplify it so it doesn't consume too much time. I hit the local supermarket on the run, not even bothering with a shopping list. When I get to the store, I know what we need for the next days, and I try to be in and out in less than half an hour.

The way Faithe and I relate is somewhat unusual. We've formed a joint venture, and we get on quite nicely together. Of course, Faithe makes my being supportive fairly easy. She throws down a challenge to me to match her courage and her positive spirit. If she were the kind of person who lay around and constantly complained, I might have been out of here ages ago. In all honesty, I don't know how I would have dealt with a different sort of person.

Most people see you as you see yourself. If you feel sorry for yourself, there's a tendency for people — even those with the best of intentions — to avoid you, to stand back, consciously or unconsciously. Conversely, a person like Faithe, who is such a positive thinker, has an army of admirers and supporters. People regularly call up to see how she's doing. If they ask Faithe directly, she always replies, "I'm doing just fine." That's immediately followed by "And how are you?" She deflects all conversation away from her own situation. The last thing Faithe wants is to be treated as an object of pity.

Sometimes I can't help being the bad guy. I get mad, swear, blow up. I even storm out of the house — especially when the tension gets the better of me. There have been times when I've blown up at Faithe. Predictably, she seems to take it in context, rather than negatively. She certainly doesn't enjoy it and occasionally breaks into tears, but there's an implied acceptance. She knows I don't do it intentionally. She says I am normal and seems relieved that I'm not overly protective of her. It's hard to stay mad at someone like that.

I can get pretty "Type A" at times, and if I constantly had to walk on eggs I'm not sure I could handle my present role. Faithe encourages me to "escape" once or twice a year. Living with and taking care of anyone 24 hours a day, 7 days a week, can be draining. That's why my adventure holidays are so important. I recently spent several weeks walking in Vietnam. The main objective is to get away from the life I normally lead and be someplace where I can go at my own speed, do my own thing, be totally selfish and self-absorbed, and come home exhausted. These holidays are often really good; other times they're not. But I'm always eager to return home.

I believe my occasional absence is good for Faithe too. Obviously, she copes better when I'm around than when I'm not, because I know what she needs more than anyone else does, like where she may have left her glasses or her book or when she needs a helping arm. But it's also important for her self-esteem to cope without me now and then.

When Faithe does feel down, I try to give her a little pep talk. I usually can sense when it's time to say nice things, and I know when it's not time to say nice things. Sometimes it's helpful when I'm sympathetic; sometimes it helps if I'm the bad guy — storming off or slamming doors.

We've found that it's important for each of us to reach out to different friends and to have separate interests and activities as well as those we share. As Faithe's mobility diminished, she had to give up activities that involved physical strength. So she considered various alternatives; one of them was bridge. When we first met years ago, she was a wretched bridge player. I had played bridge competitively throughout my college and navy years. When she mentioned her interest in bridge, I made a decision not to join her. Faithe took lessons on her own and now has her own circle of bridge friends. Since we do many things together, it's great that she has that for herself.

Many people in Faithe's circumstances might be tempted to lie around and wallow in self-pity. Anyone who wants a decent quality of life can't afford to do that. It's easy to ask "Why me?" That's a waste of time. Each day is too valuable. Faithe and I try to make the most of life one day at a time.

I'm sure there will be grim times ahead, but as long as we have a bit of forewarning and they're not too dramatic, I'm confident we can deal with them. We've learned there's no point in panicking because it doesn't help.

These days I believe in having short-term goals. The longer-term is too hard to gauge, and we could easily be drawn into "worst case" scenarios. I certainly didn't start out with this philosophy. I was a businessman whose job included long-range planning, goal setting and working out steps to achieve those goals. I always tried to anticipate what might lie beyond the horizon. I now invert that process and try to avoid pointless speculation.

I don't view myself as a caregiver for Faithe, because we are partners. It may be a cliché, but we truly are in this together. I feel good knowing she appreciates me and what I'm doing. Although my role as her partner is a strong influence in my life, it does not totally dominate it. I also have my own life to lead, and I must remain aware of my needs as well as Faithe's if I'm to avoid feeling burdened.

I've mellowed a lot since I've entered this new partnership with Faithe. Superficially, it may look like I'm doing everything and that she's not doing anything — just being taken care of. But it isn't that way at all. Her efforts regularly exceed mine. I fully appreciate the huge amount of energy required when Faithe does even the simplest things. I make a big deal about hating to clean the pots and pans. So Faithe does those for me, and it makes her feel good to be able to do them for me. Of course, I try to make sure I don't leave too many of them. It may seem like a tiny thing, but it's really appreciated. It's also important that she has a sense that she's not totally dependent or passive.

A couple nights ago I came down with a rotten cold; I felt awful. Although it was very difficult and a lot of work for Faithe, she prepared a meal for me. I appreciated it all the more because I realized how much effort she made. Sometimes it's heartbreaking to see how hard it is for her to do the things she could do so easily before.

If anyone hypothetically had posed my present situation to me a few years ago, I wouldn't have had a clue how I could have handled it. I don't think of myself as a "new man" or a "revised person," but I have learned that I can deal with most things. Of course, I'm not sure how we'll handle everything five years hence, but we'll manage somehow. As long as changes occur gradually, we should be able to make minor course corrections and adjustments as we go along.

Down deep I feel that Faithe's life is my life too. I find myself doing things that I wouldn't have done if I didn't have to worry about her. It's been an interesting experience because so much is new to me. Obviously, I'm responding positively to this situation, and there is a challenge and a certain amount of "job satisfaction" that I enjoy.

Of uppermost importance for me are Faithe the person, my relationship with her and my strong belief that we can and must make it work. Her spirit and positive attitude help make that possible. She's a delightful person to be around, and she deals with things very pleasantly. So I respond to Faithe, and she enhances my life and gives it added purpose.

Attitude is the principal thing in life. It is not the conditions in life which change life for us, but mostly it is our attitude toward life and its conditions upon which depends our happiness or unhappiness.

– Hazrat Inayat Khan

Faithe is one of the best examples I know of someone who has healed by choosing to "change the picture" of her difficulty. Although she still talks optimistically about the day "they find a cure for MS," her cheerfulness and courage are not dependent on that. She maintains a remarkably positive attitude and sees the bright side of her disability and life.

Sometimes healing begins when we choose to accept unchangeable, debilitating conditions as a learning experience and an opportunity to discover our sources of support and coping strategies. The decision to stay in charge of our lives as much as possible and to refuse to be victims are two important components of the healing process.

Although one might have expected that a Type-A workaholic spouse would not have been able to handle the difficulties of Faithe's illness, Jud has been strengthened by her restorative disposition. He too has adopted a positive outlook on their situation.

Faithe and Jud's optimistic story teaches us about the importance of choosing to turn a crisis into an opportunity and having the desire to rise above one's problems. Certainly a positive attitude is one of the most significant ingredients in any healing process. The joint healing story of Faithe and Jud is living proof.

Paul

Tower of Gratitude

I wake up every day aware that I could be dead. But I have the gift of life.
So I live each moment gratefully and intentionally.   – Paul

Long before I got to know Paul as a friend and colleague, I saw him serving as an acolyte at the Cathedral of St. John the Divine. He looked dignified and peaceful — almost ethereal — as he carried the elegant candles in the procession to the altar.

Not long after that, I started researching possibilities for working in a hospice program in New York City. I was told the best person to talk about hospice was Paul, the serene acolyte. He was absolutely dedicated to hospice work and viewed sharing people's dying process as a privilege, a special gift that was deeply rewarding for him. He was full of wonderful stories, helpful insights and valuable information. His enthusiasm was utterly contagious, and I signed up for hospice training.

At our first meeting, Paul told me that he was HIV positive and that he had embraced this disease into his life.

Paul

I grew up in a tiny little town in the Ozarks of Missouri. For 47 years, until the day he died, my father served as the only medical doctor in a 30-mile radius of our community. He made house calls and was up day and night taking care of people.

My parents and their families were all very religious — an intense mid-western Lutheranism. Religion was the fabric of the day and many of my relatives were in some kind of church work. It was almost like the air we breathed. Because I was artistic and musical, I started studying music. But when my grandmother died abruptly of a heart attack, I went into a major crisis about what I really wanted to do and what I should do. Out of that trauma, I decided to become a pastor and, after seminary, served for twelve years in Jacksonville, Florida.

In 1971, I started getting interested in death and dying work after a memorable death of Ora, a very unhappy older woman at my church. When she became seriously ill and was placed in a nursing home, she was totally distressed and inconsolable. Often the nurses called me in the middle of the night to come settle Ora. After a number of these events, I moved her into my house, as it just seemed easier. Members of the congregation helped me with the nursing care. After about six weeks, she died peacefully in my home.

Death and dying issues became increasingly important in my ministry after the experience with Ora. Although there was no place to study it, I began to incorporate the concepts and principles of hospice and death and dying deep into my own self. Eventually I went into hospice work. Little did I know how well they would serve me later in my own life.

In 1993, while I was living in Washington, DC, I noticed I had a strange skin rash. I was strongly suspicious that it was related to HIV. In those days, people with AIDS were still dying like flies, and AZT was the only drug being used. I went immediately for a test.

As I waited to hear my results, I watched the way people were called into the office for their results. Those who had tested negative went first. Those who were positive were sent to a counselor. I knew I had tested positive when I was told to go to a counselor's office.

It was a Friday evening when I left the clinic with the results. I went straight home and right to bed. I needed to stay in bed — almost like a symbolic death. I didn't get up until Monday morning when it was time to go to work. I felt very tired and winded. I didn't really know what this would mean, but I was certain it would be a total change of my life. As I lay on my bed, I looked out the window where I could see green leaves on the trees. Somehow that seemed encouraging.

Over the weekend I let the news sink in. I knew I would get on with things when I got up. It was exhausting knowing I was on the HIV path. I had been there with many others in the 1980s; lots of my friends were already dead. I had watched them and supported them along the way. I had a pretty clear idea of what that meant. But I wasn't really frightened. What was there to be frightened of? The news itself was the worst.

When you're infected, you get a whole new identity, a new persona — especially if you take on the stigma that is implied with the disease. It's like an overlay and it penetrates through everything.

Although I'm everything I always was, as soon as people know I'm HIV positive, that's often the first and only thing they see — everything else about me fades. They have no sense of what my life is like, who I am, what my values are. The main thing they focus on is my diagnosis and a set of assumptions around that.

It takes a lot of work to hold on to the truth that I am not a virus, not a disease. I am the person I always was. There's just one more thing added onto what was always there. The important thing is to plant that truth internally rather than respond to how people from the external world perceive me.

Before my diagnosis, I led countless support groups for diagnosed people. That was advantageous for me. Being deeply involved in life has been one of the most important things in helping me live successfully with my illness. Not being on the sidelines of life is critical.

When the AIDS epidemic started, it was absolutely terrifying to almost everyone. No one knew how the disease was transmitted. Could you get it from mosquitoes or a swimming pool or a toilet seat or eating utensils? From the beginning in the very early '80s, I just plunged in and began working with people who needed help. I heard hundreds of stories of what people had lived through. All that volunteer time I had invested was not wasted. Later when it was my turn, that richness came to help me.

Initially I did not tell my sons about my diagnosis. I wanted to be ready. Years later when I finally did tell them, they handled it quite comfortably and to this day they still do.

Telling someone you're HIV positive is very different from telling them you're ill or you've been injured. Immediately you see the look on someone's face that says "You're dead." Early on when I told some colleagues at my work about my status, there was a discernible difference in how they dealt with me — like I was written off, while they were getting on with their lives. I didn't need that. After that experience, I mainly told people who were infected and very few others.

In the 1980s, many of the young people with whom I worked were in their 20s and 30s. They seemed to be standing in quicksand as they tried to find their identity and deal with their diagnosis at the same time. The stigma of the disease was horrible then, and often families disowned them. Some were thrown out of apartments. It was difficult for them to find anything constructive in this because they were so fragile, so vulnerable, so feared.

Coming into this situation when I was already in my 50s had advantages. I wasn't just a kid trying to sort out everything without any resources. If it had happened when I was much younger, I'm confident I would have died. By the time I was diagnosed, I had already worked through a whole slew of tough psychological and spiritual issues. I had some skills from my training in Gestalt and Jungian work that gave me some ground to stand on and a different perspective. And I had a spiritual center; I didn't need to try to find one.

In Gestalt the focus is on the here and now. For me "the here and now" meant I had to find out what my status was and how to get decent health care. AZT was the only known drug then, and it was being used in very high dosages. I had seen firsthand how difficult it was and how sick it made people.

At the time there was great debate about the drug AZT. Some groups counseled people not to take AZT because of fear that it actually sped up the HIV process. There was suspicion and paranoia related to the drug companies. I was certain I didn't want to start on AZT and hoped I could keep away from it as long as possible.

My first T-cell count was about 620. It should have been around 1,100 or 1,200. The T-cells are part of the immune system that destroys unwanted things like bacteria and germs in the blood. If your T-cell count is low, your immune system has less ability to fight off things like infections. People who "die of AIDS" don't really die of AIDS. Rather, their immune system is too weak and they get pneumonia, cancer and other illnesses the body can't throw off. Traditionally the marker for moving from HIV to AIDS is when your T-cell count goes down to 300. Then the language changes from HIV to AIDS. However, there is still some debate as to whether HIV is the cause of AIDS.

When I did my arithmetic, I knew I was already halfway down that road. I started testing on a regular basis and watched my T-cells go lower and lower. It was important to continue what I was already doing: watching my diet, exercising, being careful and watching my stress. That's basically how I had to manage things until I got near the end. Then AZT would be brought in like the rescue squad, and that might buy me some more time. The convention of care at the time was that AZT was saved for the very end. Certainly the philosophy of medical care for the infection has been dramatically changed in the past few years.

My life moved into my "Okay, here I am with my HIV" phase. During the first period of my adjustment, I started paying a great deal of attention to my dreams in case there was something I was repressing or not tending to or denying. I knew it would show up there. I carefully recorded all dreams in my journal, but nothing disruptive or unusual showed up. Somehow my life was moving on. Recording my dreams was a useful technique for me because it confirmed that the way I was managing my life was okay.

I started to notice that I was bruising a lot and that at times my urine was almost brown. I felt very weak. I've always been a high-energy person, so not having energy was a real indicator to me that something was wrong.

For a long time my doctor couldn't figure out what was going on. Meanwhile my symptoms kept getting worse. It was very troubling.

The T-cells are one kind of countdown. I was also doing a countdown on my spleen, one of the first lines of defense in the immune system. Somehow my spleen had been damaged or weakened by the HIV virus. It was the way the virus made an inroad into my health, and it was causing a serious crisis. I came very close to dying.

Finally I was diagnosed as having thrombocytopenia, which is a rare HIV-related event. Leave it to me to get something unusual! My spleen was malfunctioning and my platelet count was way down. There's not a cure, but there are treatments. Yet every treatment I took made me ferociously sick. At one point I spent a weekend in the emergency room, which made things worse.

When my spleen count hit 11,000 in 1996, I knew I was facing death, because a normal spleen count is somewhere in the range of 150,000 to 200,000. I was so weak it was scary. In the morning I went to work with enough energy, but by the afternoon I would feel myself sinking. I'd get home and collapse in bed too weak to get up, too weak to make supper. I could only sleep. In the morning I'd get up and try to function again. That's how I lived.

Often when I woke up in the morning, I would be bruised with big black and blue marks from the internal bleeding and lack of clotting. I had to quit shaving with a razor. If I cut myself, I would bleed and bleed and I couldn't stop it. Whenever I walked on the street, I had to walk defensively. People bumping up against me in a normal jostling would cause me to get huge bruises. Sometimes I would have to sit on the street curb because I didn't have enough energy to continue walking. It was a dreadful time.

I was being pulled down fast. I joked with my doctor, "I'm not going to live until Thanksgiving, and that's just too soon. I don't have enough time to take care of everything." The most difficult thing was that I had many things I still wanted to do, and I was afraid I wasn't going to get to do them. I had a terrible sense of the incompleteness of my life. That was really burdensome for me, but there was nothing that could be done about it. I realized that if my life ended, it would be a series of three dots . . . for all my unfinished stuff.

Finally my doctor said there was one thing left to try: taking my spleen. There was a 65 percent chance that would be successful. At the rate I was going, the odds and risks were definitely worth taking. The surgeon couldn't immediately operate on me because my platelets were too low; they needed to come up to 50,000. The only way to do that was to put me on some powerful steroids.

For three months we worked at getting me strong enough to handle the surgery. It was a very spacey time with the steroids; I felt like I was always off the wall. I worked out at the gym every day to get more energy. I tried to build myself up to my optimal level of health before I entered the hospital.

It was a troublesome time for me. There was a real possibility I wouldn't make it through the procedure, so I began preparing for my death. I told myself I had done everything I could. I made sure my will was up to date. I wrote letters to people who were close to me with instructions to mail them should I die. I took care of those kinds of details.

But no matter what I said or did, the overwhelming feeling that it was just too soon would not go away. Over and over I said, "I can't die. I don't have time to die." There were many things I wanted to do related to my professional work in hospice and its future, including my involvement in the development of the palliative care movement.

On the personal side, if I ever had the opportunity to reach old age — whatever that might mean — I wanted to return to my music. I also hoped to do some writing and poetry, which I haven't been able to do in this season of my life because my professional side is full of many projects I need to see through. There was an urgent feeling of "Wait, I must do these things." I was fiercely determined that somehow I would get through this ordeal and I would live long enough to have the chance to do them.

Also there were my relationships with my sons, who were then 26 and 29. I wanted to see them into full adulthood. I didn't need to travel around the world and see the Acropolis or the Pyramids or whatever else. But there were people I wanted to be with and things I wanted to do.

Kathy, a close friend who is a nurse in Jacksonville, came up to provide support to me during my surgery and recovery. I realized I would be too out of it to determine what I did or didn't need, or to recognize good or bad care, or to know if something was a crisis or not. As a nurse, Kathy would know these things. So when she offered to come to help, I accepted her offer — one of the rare times I've allowed someone to do that. It has always been difficult for me to accept help. But this time, when Kathy said she would be my advocate, I had no doubt that it was the right thing. "That's great. Come," was my response.

Kathy went through the whole process with me — being admitted to the hospital, the surgery, my recovery in the hospital — until I went home. Her assistance was critical, especially the emotional and spiritual support she provided. It was a relief knowing I had someone I could depend on, and it made a huge difference in my mental health. I don't know if I could have gotten through it without Kathy.

The surgery was successful, and my T-cell count immediately and automatically went up to 950 from about 350. It was like someone had waved a magic wand over me. Not only did my T-cell count go up, but the removal of my spleen caused my platelet count to move into the normal range. The surgery corrected things and that has held.

After the spleen correction, my doctor and I had a long talk about the best course of action. Should we just be thankful that I had returned to the top of the line? Should we test every three months to see if there might be a slow decline? Should we just watch that? Or should we use the new drugs and try to contain the virus? There was a whole new range of drugs available, with the multiple drug therapy offering a new standard of care.

We decided to try the drugs, and I started on what is called the new highly aggressive anti-retral viral therapy (HAART). There are now fourteen available drugs that can be used, and the next generation of drugs is being developed and tested. If these drugs don't work, there is a good chance there will be something else.

Going on the drug therapy was an interesting change for me because initially I had been against going on any drugs. To have used the drugs in the beginning would have implied a depth of admission I wasn't prepared to make then. I wanted to hold off as long as possible, a way of holding on to my non-AIDS life.

When I went through the crisis with my spleen, things got blasted out of the water, and many earlier ideas became irrelevant. The fact that I now take seventeen pills a day — or however many it is — no longer matters. I am at a different place. If I can keep my T-cell count up and my viral load down by taking all the medications, that's okay now. I can live with that but I can't live with the uncertainty of just watching.

Of course, there's a crapshoot with all of this. No one knows how long these drugs will last or benefit me, or if I've shot my load early. We haven't been living with these drugs long enough to know. But I have a relative confidence that there may be something in the new class of drugs that will work for me.

It's difficult to manage these drugs in the best of all worlds. I can only take some of the drugs when I eat. Others can't be taken with food. I have to pay absolute careful attention to this. I don't dare screw up. I can't miss a dosage, or the virus starts to build capacity against the medicine, and that particular drug may not work. Then I have to go through what is called salvage therapy.

Knowing that I can never take anything for granted with these medications is a kind of stress. I always have to think things through in advance; I have to anticipate the day and its schedule; I need to be prepared in case I get caught in a bind or there is an emergency at work. I carry an entire set of pills with me all the time. I learned that the hard way after I got stuck a couple of times. The viral load immediately started to creep up, and the T-cells went down. So far I've been successful in pushing it back down again. I just can't afford to play Russian roulette with this. The stakes are too high.

In terms of side effects, I had bad diarrhea for about a month and a half when I first started on the drugs. Every now and then it flares up, and I have another episode. But I've never been really nauseated. Different people experience these drugs in different ways. A close friend of mine could not stay on this medication because he became violently ill with diarrhea and vomiting.

The persistent symptom that I have is neuropathy in my feet, making it very painful and sometimes hard to walk. Often it feels like I have slabs in my feet and I can't feel hot or cold on the bottom of them. The insides of my feet sometimes feel prickly or heavy — like I have 50-pound weights on each foot. They are always uncomfortable, whether I'm awake or asleep. I take some medication to counteract that. That's where it has me, but it's something I can live with. Otherwise I feel really "normal."

On my last tests, my T-cells were at about 800 and my viral load was around 200. So I'm in a relatively good place. That doesn't mean the virus has gone away; it just means it's being held at bay. In the current way of understanding, it's the goal to try to keep the viral load under 5,000. Of course, the best situation would be to have it suppressed and not detectable.

The downward push of my viral load has been due to my own immune system working, not because of any change in my medications. It is slowly suppressing the virus with the help of the medications. That's very encouraging. Yes, I believe I'm going to be around for quite a while now. In fact I feel better than I have for a long time!

There are many important things I do to keep myself healthy and healing. I make certain I adhere to my medication schedule. Every time I take my medications, I do a guided imagery. I talk to my pills and give them very clear instructions what to do. The virus is very sneaky so I have to remind them not to take anything for granted, not to get lazy on the job and to keep their eyes out for any problems. I also talk to my immune system all the time, just like I talk to my body at the gym. It's a great technique.

I take a number of nutritional supplements to keep my immune system strong, including high-powered vitamins. The medications suppress many vitamins, so I take supplements to counter balance that.

I'm also on a high protein diet to support my exercises, keep my body mass and not lose weight. About five times a week I go to the gym, which is good for me physically, of course, but also mentally and spiritually. It gives me distance from my work and its stresses, and I see a whole different group of people at the gym with whom I socialize.

For my spiritual side, I write in my journal every day and do my guided imagery. If I'm under a lot of stress, I take myself to one of my favorite spots to relax, take in the smells and feel the ambiance of the place. Sometimes I send a healing orb of light through my body.

In 1971, I became involved with meditation — an incredibly useful skill for me. I combine Zen meditation with weight lifting. It's a wonderful endeavor to be conscious but not thinking. I enjoy getting into that place where I have a calm feeling of "no mind, just awareness." Doing this is helping me be well.

One of the most important learnings of my life is that I have choices. An experience simply is; it's not right or wrong, it's not good or bad, it just is. Whatever it is, it is. It's my choice to make it whatever I want it to be. It can be awful, bad and terrible, if that's what I want it to be. Or it can be laced with potential, miracle and wonder. My decision makes it that way. An experience doesn't exist somewhere outside of me. It's within me, and its meaning itself is inside me.

Living with the HIV disease could be terrible, and for a lot of people it is horrible. I just choose for it not to be. That's different from saying "it's easy." Yet I feel it's within my range of choices to make it what I want it to be. I have made the decision to live as well as I have the power and ability to live. I can't take away the HIV, but it's not a black cloud hanging over my head. It's just a fact of my life. I try to live with it well and consciously.

My life is very much driven by the HIV, but in a constructive way that is healing rather than destructive. Certainly it could pull me down and force me to focus on the things I have lost as a consequence of being infected. But I don't have time to feel sorry for myself, I don't have time to feel resentful, I don't have time to feel like I've lost a lot — because I haven't. I feel I have gained far, far more than I've lost.

I wake up every day aware that I could be dead. But I have the gift of life. So I live each moment incredibly intentionally. I know so many people who are walking around and are "dead." They have no joy in life and are full of poison and negativity. They are not living. They're throwing their life away without realizing it. I feel sorry for them, but I don't feel sorry for myself. I feel fortunate, so blessed.

I don't have time for people who are full of complaints. When I ride the elevator at the hospital and hear conversations of complainers, I sometimes want to say, "Half the people in this world would be very happy to be in your condition. Get over it. Get a life and start living it." If someone needs to complain, well, okay. Just don't do it on my time.

Anyone can be negative. That takes no great gift! You can just open your eyes and look at the world and be negative. Or you can find beauty and feel positive about it.

A friend of mine who was dying of AIDS in 1985 told me just a few months before he died, "You know, Paul, AIDS saved my life." People who aren't living from inside this may look at someone with HIV or AIDS and think of them as having a curse or a death sentence. But I say "no, no, no" to that. This illness came into my life. Perhaps I needed a lesson. Now it's my choice to make something positive out of it.

Every day it's amazing to be alive. Whatever the day holds, whatever it is, it's good. In the face of death, intentional living is what I've learned to do. I don't take anything for granted. I take the moments I'm given as extraordinary. I love this moment, this day, this time of my life. I'm so thankful to be alive.

Healing requires that we reach out . . . to something that gives us new life, new hope, new pleasure. Healing is the process of refusing to be wounded.

– Joan Chittister

From the first time I met with Paul, he talked about being grateful for having been given the gift of a full and joyful life. Even when he told me he was HIV positive, I never once had the feeling that he felt sorry for himself or that he was looking for sympathy.

Unquestionably Paul has a lot of resources available to him, but he also has something we all need: mature inner resources. He is well grounded in useful spiritual practices, all of which help him deal with his situation. Living with the HIV disease can be humiliating and distressing, but Paul shows strength and courage in facing his illness and peoples' negative responses to it. He has chosen to live life full steam ahead and to use the illness to expand rather than constrict his horizons. In the face of death, every moment is extraordinary for him, and he is grateful to be alive.

Whenever we choose to be deeply involved in life, make an effort to keep our bodies and spirits in shape, set new goals for ourselves and find beauty in the world, the healing process will remain alive within us. And if, like Paul, we don't have time to feel sorry for ourselves and we feel grateful for the gift of life, we may find we will gain more than we lose.

DONNA AND KIEU
Towers of Love

Fear and lack of trust made Kieu shut down. When she was given love, she quickly responded. Her love has helped Phil and me learn some profound lessons from the challenge of infertility. — Donna

Donna is an optimistic, high-energy, lover-of-life woman, someone I thoroughly enjoy. When Donna came to work for the Health Unit at Save the Children, I was the director of the Asia/Pacific Region. The quality of her professional support to the health programs I supervised received rave reviews and requests for her return.

As we worked together over the years, I learned of Donna's deep desire to have a child. But before her wish could be fulfilled, she and her husband Phil struggled with years of disappointment and difficulty as they faced the challenge of infertility.

Years later when I was working at Christian Children's Fund (CCF) as director of International Programs, I hired Donna as a consultant.

Her first assignment was tough, one that I hesitated asking her to do but knew she could handle: a healthcare assessment in Somalia where a nasty war was going on. Much later, after she had completed the consultation, we learned what a mixed blessing it had been — both a treacherous assignment and a lifesaver.

Donna

Working in international public health in the developing world, I saw tremendous needs: children without parenting, rejected children, unwanted pregnancies. When Phil proposed marriage to me, I told him I would never have children, that we would adopt children because there were too many unwanted children on an already overpopulated planet.

During my early years in public health, people often asked, "Are you married? How many children do you have?" When I'd say "none," they'd ask what was wrong with our marriage. They couldn't understand why we didn't have children, so I'd tell them about family planning. In developing countries, most women believe family planning should only be used after you've had children.

It wasn't long before my maternal instincts started to rise. It seemed important to be a mother — not only for my own spiritual, emotional and physical life, but also for my work, since I was teaching about maternal health and breastfeeding. How could people believe me if I had never done it myself?

One day I told Phil, "Let's try to have a child." But he was reluctant so we waited a few more years. We were living in Indonesia when we finally tried to conceive, and it proved to be very difficult. We struggled with infertility for almost five years. Infertility introduces enormous stress on a relationship, and there is a sense of inadequacy, blame, questions about your own togetherness and how you may not work as a couple since you can't even have a child. So many intense issues surface.

One by one my friends got pregnant, but I didn't. Daily I'd see women in my work who had six or seven kids and were pregnant again, and miserable about it. "Why?" I wondered. "I just want one child."

I realized I had a lot of inner work to do before I was ready to be a mother. I began to look deeper into who I was and why this was happening. It became clear that I needed to have a greater self-awareness and self-knowledge to be prepared to attract a soul. I've come to believe that when things go well, parents attract the soul they need. So pregnancy is on a soul level, and things tend to fall into place naturally once the soul has been correctly aligned. But it's not always easy to wait for that.

Now I'm grateful for those years of waiting. It was important to do some homework and to wake up to who and what I was. I got a whole new understanding about conceiving children. I had expected to get pregnant while I was running around saving the world, changing time zones, not nurturing myself, having no normal periods or cycles, and getting my hormones out of whack. Needless to say, I wasn't home enough with my husband to get pregnant. Then too when I was stressed from my work, I didn't take care of myself, relax enough or nurture the home in my heart. I had to learn how to be quiet and tranquil and allow myself to be more maternal.

Phil and I decided to use natural therapies and healing approaches rather than high-tech interventions. Living in Asia was a perfect place to do that. We went to a Chinese doctor for herbs since Phil and I were both sub-fertile. A powerful Indian healer introduced me to behavioral kinesiology, aromatherapy, Bach flower remedies and Reiki. We tried massage, reflexology and acupuncture. I also did some spiritual work that led me to a higher awareness of my being and how I could be a better mother.

For a period of time, my desire to get pregnant became an obsession. It was hard to keep it in perspective. Eventually I came to a deeper understanding and acceptance, and I began to relax.

While we were on home leave in California, Phil admitted he was getting frustrated that we had not tried any high-tech procedures. Finally, in fairness to him, I agreed we would try an in vitro fertilization (IVF).

But when Joy called and asked me to do some consulting work in Somalia, without hesitation I said "yes." Then I told Phil about this new assignment. "You really don't want a baby," was his response. "There's a war going on in Somalia. You're not going to get pregnant. Why are you doing this?" All I could say was, "I really have to do this. I'll go to Singapore and start the IVF process as soon as I come back."

So I went to Somalia to the most "on-edge" job I had ever done. I had never been in the middle of a full-scale war. I had only worked with the aftermath of it. During the month I was there, I had little sleep, limited nutrition and was in constant fear. There were mines, guns and bombs going off everywhere. A Somali bodyguard was with me the entire time, and we traveled by armed convoys. I was terrified.

When I returned through Singapore, I went to the IVF doctor and announced: "I'm ready. I don't have my period yet because I had a lot of stress during the last month. I'm not using herbs anymore, so you can start me on the drugs. I need to get my period so we can begin this process."

The doctor explained that he had to do a pregnancy test first. I just laughed at him. "Don't waste your time and my money. It's obvious why my period was delayed. I'm not pregnant." He insisted he had to do the test because it was the law in Singapore. When he told me the test results, I couldn't believe it. I was pregnant. "You must have switched the urine," I declared. "No, it's yours," he insisted. "Go get an ultrasound." When I did, I was stunned to see a tiny grain of rice pulsating in my abdomen. I had conceived just before I left for Somalia.

It occurred to me that had I not been in Somalia I would have gone straight to Singapore, where the doctors might not have been able to detect such an early pregnancy. I may have been pumped up with hormones, and what was already growing in me may have died. That assignment probably saved our child's life. How ironic that going to a war zone to help others at high risk of being killed allowed new life to come into our lives.

As I thought about being near that dreadful war during the early part of my pregnancy, I was frightened that the poor little soul inside me had seen the worst of the world from the start. Now I think it gave my son Kai an amazing resiliency and strength.

With the pregnancy, everything started changing for us. My changes were more spiritual than physical, which allowed my body to adjust to my inner world. We needed to be prepared because being parents is such a sacred task.

When Kai was four, he started saying he wanted a little sister. We were already trying to get pregnant again — without success. "If you and daddy don't make a baby," he told us one day, "why don't we go buy one?" From the mouths of babes!

We knew firsthand that in many developing countries there aren't adequate resources for all the children. Why should we bring another child onto the planet? It was time to apply for adoption. We started sifting through the hundreds of agencies listed on the Internet and finally contacted a local agency.

We wanted a girl and were willing to take an older child. Because many behaviors and attitudes are set in the first three years of life, we hoped she would be less than eighteen months so we could have some influence on her development. Vietnam was a culture we both loved and appreciated, and I had always been drawn to Vietnamese people, admiring and appreciating their culture and their adaptability. We decided we wanted a Vietnamese girl.

In January we started the paperwork. For one year we underwent what I call a "soul pregnancy." At times it was burdensome and difficult: filling out papers, getting fingerprints and police reports, writing up petitions and essays, and going through interviews with a social worker. Since it was all in the interest of child protection, we willingly underwent the rigorous investigations. We were asked questions about our spirituality, how we planned to raise our children, our financial and other strategies in life.

In retrospect, I'm glad we went through that process. All parents should be given this kind of questioning and thoughtful preparation before bringing children into the world. Too often people have children without even thinking about it.

About nine months into the process, we got word that the agency had identified a child for us. They sent us a name and a birth date for a little girl — not much to base a decision on, but we felt it was enough.

She was almost twelve months old, and her name was Kieu Ngoc Thuy. The name Ngoc means jade, and Kieu means bridge.

I told my family about the meaning of Kieu's name: "She's a bridge between Vietnam and America." My sister reminded me that our last name Sillan is a direct translation in Finnish for bridge. With the same meaning for our names, I was sure she was our girl, part of our family.

Kieu is from the Muong hill tribe in the north of Vietnam, which also seemed appropriate. I had worked with hill tribe people in a refugee camp in Thailand. The experience was also part of my preparation for her arrival into our family.

About the same time, I did a consultation in Cambodia. Although I was right next door to Vietnam, the adoption agency wouldn't allow me to visit Kieu. They were very protective of the process, and we were only permitted to do things on their schedule.

Kieu had her first birthday on September 24 while I was in Cambodia. In a beautiful temple overlooking Phnom Penh, I celebrated her birthday. I bought incense, flowers and two birds, one for Kai and one for Kieu. I set the birds free at the temple. This is a Buddhist ritual symbolizing the freeing of souls to create good karma.

In November we heard that we had to be in Hanoi in two weeks. I almost panicked because it was close to the holidays and flights were full. After everything was set up, we received another message: "Sorry, you can't come to Vietnam now. Kieu's paperwork is not finished. You may have to wait another month." Somehow this felt okay; the time must not have been right. My friends couldn't understand why I wasn't upset that my daughter was stuck in an orphanage in Vietnam. But I didn't mind waiting because I knew this was not something to force.

A week later another message came: "You must be in Hanoi within five days." Even though it was difficult to arrange, I trusted there was a reason.

Because Kai was in school, I flew alone to Vietnam. Phil and Kai were to join me a week later. After years of seeing children in need of caring in many countries and wanting to take them home with me, this time I was actually going to do it. It seemed strange that I was on my way to pick up a little human being to bring into our family.

The agency people were at the airport when I arrived in Hanoi. They instructed me to go to a little hotel at four o'clock where I would be given my child. Fortunately, I was able to stay with a good friend living in Hanoi, who was a fantastic support for me.

It felt like I was going to the hospital to deliver my baby, and I was already almost twelve months pregnant! We had started the process of adoption on January 1, we first heard about Kieu in September before her first birthday, and I flew to Hanoi on December 7 to pick her up. Although slightly nervous, I was ready to "deliver."

At four o'clock I arrived at the hotel where adoptive parents stayed. It was on a busy, neon-lit street, and it was tiny and inexpensive because the adoption process is tremendously costly for families.

I'll never forget how I felt as I stepped into the lobby of that hotel and was handed a tiny child. "Here's your baby," they said as they took off. Although I had lived in Asia for years, had been in Vietnam many times before and had mothering experience with my own son, I felt ill prepared and in a state of shock. With me were women and men who had never had children, had never been in Asia or Vietnam, and were suddenly handed a child in a strange country. It must have been even more frightening for them.

When I delivered Kai, I experienced some of the same feelings I did at Kieu's "delivery." As Kai looked at me, I felt like he was asking, "Are you my mother?" I looked into his eyes and asked, "Are you my son?" I felt a sense of loneliness and awe for him because he seemed alone and old and because he had traveled such a long distance.

When they put Kieu in my arms, I had similar feelings. Although I had never met her before, it was clear that this underweight, feverish and pale little child was my daughter. She seemed old, wise and lonely, and they were just giving her to me, a total stranger. I looked down at her and asked, "Are you my daughter?" And she looked up at me with her stone face as though asking, "Are you my mother? And what's a mother?" It was uncanny to feel such an instant bond with her. When I looked at another girl the same age as Kieu, adopted the very same day, I had absolutely no feeling for her and no sense that she was my daughter.

Kieu had on a little white hat and cotton clothes. Her face and body were covered with scabies and her arms were bloody where she had scratched the extremely itchy invisible mites.

I had expected to get a toddler who was walking and talking. Instead I was given an infant who could not sit up, stand, walk or talk, and she was half as big as I had expected. She weighed about fourteen pounds and was the size of a four- to six-month-old baby. Another woman received a four-month-old child who was the same size as my fifteen-month-old daughter. That was worrisome, but I knew it was okay.

Kieu had an unbelievably stone face about her; she was totally stoic. She would not crack a smile, shed a tear or respond to anything I did. Her look seemed to say: "Don't mess with me. I'm an adult!" In some ways she seemed older and stronger than me. At my friend's house I held her and tried to give her love, but there was absolutely no feedback.

Initially Kieu didn't want to eat or drink, and she didn't want anything to do with anyone. So I just carried around this fourteen-pound stone. In the mornings I walked with her to the market for noodle soup and all over the streets of Hanoi.

I had been nervous about how the Vietnamese might respond to Kieu's adoption. I wondered if they would be upset that Americans were taking a child away from their country. I was relieved that they seemed happy and receptive to us. They often asked: "Is she Vietnamese? Are you taking her to America?"

When I had packed my bag for Vietnam, I had put in it some stuffed animals, toys and books that I thought Kieu could play with. But when I set them in front of her, she turned her head away in disgust as though she couldn't bear to see them. "What are those things? Get them out of my life." Kieu didn't know how to play. She couldn't see a stuffed animal as something to cuddle or love. So I put them away.

Kieu just lay there totally shut down. She only gave me one tiny smile exactly 24 hours from the time she was first handed to me in the hotel. It was something, a small glimmer of hope. Then she closed down again.

As the days passed, I knew I would continue to love Kieu, but I hoped I wouldn't use up all my resources in the process. Although I believe love is infinite, at the same time one needs to be replenished or get some kind of feedback. But I wasn't getting anywhere with her. I was afraid that Kieu might have completely shut down emotionally and was already a hard-shelled adult.

When I took Kieu to a doctor in Hanoi, she was given an HIV and HEP-B test. Although we had asked for this information prior to picking her up, we had blindly accepted her without the tests. In the end, we trusted that she'd be okay, and she was.

Kieu had a severe case of scabies, which I caught since we slept together, and it's highly contagious. It was terrible to see how much she suffered from it, constantly scratching and tearing at her flesh, but she didn't cry. She had probably lived with the disease all her life. I couldn't tolerate the scabies and was totally miserable, endlessly scratching myself. It was probably good that I got a case, since for years I had treated babies with the disease and had no clue what it was like. Now I will be more understanding.

On the fourth day, we were to go to Kieu's village for a "giving and receiving ceremony." Kieu's mother had been invited to the ceremony, but she didn't show up. I had heard of an incident where a Vietnamese mother came for her child's giving and receiving ceremony, and the American adoptive mother felt guilty about taking the child from its natural mother. But the Vietnamese mother told her: "Because I love her, I can give my daughter to you."

The Vietnamese are very practical people, and they lovingly give a child away to have a better quality of life. Kieu's mother, a 27-year-old rice farmer, had Kieu out of wedlock, an embarrassing situation in Asia. She could not afford to raise her since she already had a four-year-old son. She kept Kieu the first three months and likely breastfed her. I'm confident Kieu had her mother's love then.

By the time Phil and Kai joined us, Kieu was beginning to soften and cry a little. But she was still fairly shut down. She started changing and opening to us shortly after their arrival. Once she did, she must have had positive feelings and wanted more. It was as though she learned how to pull our heartstrings, and we responded by giving her more love. How quickly the power of love worked!

We promoted Kai to the role of big brother with the job of teaching his new sister how to laugh and cry. Obviously Kieu didn't cry because it had not worked for her in the past and no one had responded to her cries. If no one seems to love you, it's not okay to cry. Perhaps our unconditional love helped open her locked heart, and she began to feel and express her emotions. Slowly, slowly she realized it was okay to laugh and cry. We were relieved to hear Kieu's tiny cries and laughter after she had been so stoic.

When Kieu first refused to eat, it felt like a rejection of my motherly love. Having dealt with malnutrition for many years, I desperately wanted to nurture and feed her in every way — especially through her stomach. When she finally started to receive our love, she also began to accept and relish food. Then she couldn't stop eating and ate mounds of food — especially vegetables and salty Vietnamese foods. I had to be careful not to feed her so much that she would get sick.

Phil and I were certain we'd be better parents if we knew something about Kieu's background. But as new adoptive parents, we were not supposed to visit her orphanage, which is run by an American woman with Vietnamese staff. They probably were concerned that parents might be shocked at the extremely poor conditions. Since I've worked in developing countries most of my adult life, almost nothing shocks me.

When we arrived at the orphanage, we were greeted with open arms. The Vietnamese caretakers seemed grateful to see Kieu again. The place had only five caregivers for seventy children. In each crib five children lay side by side on wooden slabs with straw mats. Many of the children had runny noses and thin hair. They were ridden with scabies and suffered from malnutrition. The newborn babies, who were mostly female, were wrapped like little papooses lying in a kind of production line.

The children had no place to play. They were not allowed on the concrete floor, since it was too cold and sanitation would be a problem. There were no toys except for a few stuffed animals locked behind a glass, probably considered too good to play with.

The children stayed in their cribs and were discouraged from walking since there weren't enough staff to run after them. I realized the back of Kieu's head was flat because she had been lying almost immobile for the last year. Being with four other children in a crib, however, was more humane and better than solitary confinement in a single crib with no human contact. They could at least touch one another and have some kind of connection to each other. No solid food was given to the children since the staff couldn't feed all of the children at once. At fifteen months, Kieu had never chewed a solid piece of food; she only had formula in a propped bottle.

Seeing this helped us understand why Kieu was lethargic and couldn't sit up. She kept falling over, didn't try to get up, crawl or walk. Usually babies put things in their mouths as a way of exploring and getting to know the world, but Kieu didn't. A volunteer from another orphanage told me that children's hands were slapped if they put something in their mouths because it might be dirty and cause more illness. Under the circumstances, Kieu was as healthy as she could be.

In the end, visiting the orphanage was a relief, not a shock. Seeing where Kieu had lived helped us understand some of her symptoms and behaviors. The children had to become self-reliant like little adults, because there weren't enough people to care for them. We also realized we'd taken Kieu away from her community, and we wondered if she felt abandoned or that she was abandoning them. We were glad that we had chosen to pick her up in her country rather than meet her at the San Francisco Airport.

Often I wish I could go inside Kieu's mind and know what she is thinking or feeling. Of course, she can't express it now, but I believe this is etched on her soul. Someone said Kieu would never remember any of this. However, I will encourage her to recall the reality of her first year of life since it's part of her.

The first night in our home, Kieu seemed upset and cried for nearly 24 hours. We worried that our home might not suit her, but later we realized there were many things going on: the strangeness of the place and a release of her pent-up feelings.

It wasn't long before Kieu started smiling and doing amazing things. She watched others do something and then tried to do it herself — like trying to feed herself or putting a comb to her hair and a toothbrush in her mouth. Children who have been in institutions are often early self-feeders and more self-reliant, a matter of survival.

We realized we couldn't measure Kieu by "normal" milestones. We had to treat her where she was developmentally. She needed to reclaim lost time and go back through the baby stages she missed. Just because she was 15 months old, she didn't have to start walking. However, it wasn't long before Kieu was crawling, pulling herself up and then walking. In less than three months she went from not being able to sit up by herself to walking. Gradually she showed an interest in stuffed animals. Now she hugs and feeds them with her bottle, looks at books for long periods and tries to draw.

When I took Kieu to the local pediatricians for a medical check-up, they treated her very casually — like a local girl. Later I found a pediatrician who specialized in international adopted children and who did the entire exam in great detail, trying different cognitive tests and putting the results into a developmental framework. Since the doctor regularly dealt with institutionalized children who had been understimulated, she expected Kieu's cognitive development would be delayed. But she was surprised to see very positive results. Kieu's body was like that of a 10-month-old child and her cognitive skills were like a normal, 16-month-old. "This goes to show you the resilient power of genes," the doctor exclaimed. Very young children who have been institutionalized can eventually catch up if they are given proper food, stimulation and love.

Certainly the process of an international adoption is long and arduous, usually more difficult than a regular pregnancy. Our situation is not yet finished, and we'll be on edge until it is. Kieu has a Vietnamese passport until she is naturalized, which can take up to two years. Initially that upset me, because I wanted to bring Kieu with me to some of my overseas work. This will also limit our family's ability to travel outside the States. It was hard to imagine not being able to move around as freely. Kieu may have grounded me somewhat to our home in California, but she has also helped to ground me spiritually. Plus, I now have a much greater sense of empathy for refugees and others with green cards who have little freedom of movement.

When we first considered having a second child, there was a question in my mind: Would we love a second child as much as we loved the first? Now I know the answer: We love Kieu just as much as Kai and are grateful to have both of them. It's proof that children can come to us in different ways and we can love them whether they are through our flesh or not. I can certainly witness to that — especially after all we went through to get each one of our children. Both of our "pregnancies" were difficult, but that has made us appreciate and understand the sacredness of each child. I feel happy that we have both a biological and an adopted child.

Kieu has become my little teacher. She has helped me get a better understanding about nutrition, that it has to do with interacting and loving. Kieu has also been a teacher for Kai who initially was a bit wary and jealous of her. He may have been lonely as an only child, but now he enjoys being with her. He recently said he loves her so much he wants to marry her.

Although Kieu was not accustomed to male energy because she had no father and only female caregivers in the orphanage, she immediately responded positively to Phil, often falling asleep on his shoulder. He carried her around everywhere and was totally enamoured of her. The love between them as father and daughter has made Phil very soft.

Because Kieu seemed to fit well into each of our destinies, I wondered how the agency made decisions about which child went with whom, so I wrote them asking how children were placed. We were blown away by the answer we received:

> "Over the 25 years that I have been placing children I have frequently been asked that question. I have watched infants grow up to be so similar to their adoptive parents. I always say I have never chosen a child for anyone, and I have participated in what is divine guidance. I believe these children are "preordained" to become someone's child, and that is why it is so important that people wait for their child — not just any child. I am so happy that you got the right one."

Every day Kieu seems to grow by leaps and bounds. She's gaining weight and growing taller, she has teeth and lots of new hair, and her head is rounding out. Food alone doesn't make her grow. Love makes her grow — physically, emotionally, mentally, spiritually. I believe fear of abandonment and lack of trust made Kieu shut down. When she was given love, she quickly responded.

Kieu has truly completed our family, bringing us the gift of togetherness. Since she has come to live with us, the whole dynamic of our family has been elevated to a different level. There is a new spirit and much joy in our home. We appreciate the love she gives us along with the opportunities she offers us to love her. She is a special presence in our home — like a ray of bright sunshine.

Kieu's love has helped Phil and me to heal our wounds too — especially those of infertility. We have learned some profound lessons through the challenges of infertility and the adoption process. Both were worth the pain and trials we went through. We needed to come to an acceptance of our problems and to be more receptive to the ways of the world and how God works. I believe we didn't get pregnant again because we needed Kieu. Once we surrendered to our sense of weakness or inadequacy, we understood how lucky we were to be the stewards of such angels and how much they give us in our development as we assist them in theirs. The adoption of Kieu and her love to us are helping us grow.

Yes, love is a powerful healer.

When you touch deep understanding and love, you are healed.
— Thich Nhat Hanh

Donna and Kieu's story confirms what has often been said: Love is a powerful and miraculous healer. The quantity and quality of love that Donna and her family have poured on Kieu has reaped an enormous harvest: Kieu's transformation into a joyful, healthy child. Because healing is often interactive and involves relationships with others, the miracle of love didn't stop with Kieu; it reached her adoptive parents, who also needed healing from their disappointments and difficulties with infertility.

Kieu may not have realized that she needed healing when she was taken out of her crib in the orphanage — the only life she knew. Often we are unaware of our needs for healing, and we may push away others' efforts to help us. There is always the possibility that, like the stoic, shutdown Kieu, we just might respond to some freely-given doses of love and nurturing.

Donna and Phil learned some powerful lessons that all couples hoping to have children in their life might want to consider: that successful pregnancy, adoption and parenting are not just events to fit into a busy schedule. Rather, they are on a deeper level, requiring preparation and development of one's spiritual and authentic selves.

When I interviewed Donna, Kieu played happily with her books and toys. Later when I listened to the taped recordings of our sessions, I could hear her sweet little voice cooing some song from her heart — a heart opened and healed by the gift of love from her family.

CHARLIE

Tower of Learning

I stopped using drugs because I knew it wasn't the life I wanted to live. My nurse too was very important in my healing because she talked straight and didn't try to keep from hurting my feelings. If my feelings were hurt, I would get over it. But if I didn't do the right thing, I wouldn't. – Charlie

For several years I worked as a volunteer chaplain on the dialysis unit at Bellevue Hospital in New York City. It took weeks to learn the ropes of the unit and to acquaint myself with the patients who regularly did time on these formidable machines. With an increasing admiration for their courage, I listened to the often tragic and painful stories of my patients, trying to understand how best to support them as they endured their arduous routines.

The standard drill for many patients in the peritoneal dialysis unit is eight to twelve hours connected to a noisy machine two or three times a week. Although the hospital beds and the leather reclining easy chairs are comfortable, many patients feel like life has been severely restricted for them. They know they may be hostages to these machines for the rest of their lives.

Then one day I met Charlie. Hooked up to a machine, he greeted me with bright eyes and a big grin. With well-defined muscles in his slim arms, Charlie was dressed in groovy overalls and hiking boots. He was a bright spot in the grayish dialysis room, smiling and laughing as though all was well in his world.

Charlie

Looking back from the point of view of a man, I think we were quite well off as a family when we lived in Georgia. I had nine brothers and sisters, and sometimes we had to take turns going to school because our parents needed us to help with the sharecropping in the cotton and corn fields. Or there were times when we had to take care of the younger kids. But we had our own house and some of our own land.

We gave up everything when we left there. In New York City we had nothing. We had to start from scratch. That's when all hell broke loose. From the day we arrived in Harlem and I started going to elementary school, I saw a lot of drug use and drug selling and trading.

In a way I was in the wrong place at the wrong time. As a young adolescent from the South, I just didn't know a lot about drugs. So when I ran into different kinds of people, I wanted to be just like them, and they all seemed to be using drugs.

By the time I got into the seventh grade, I had started selling drugs, mostly heroin. At first I didn't do drugs myself. But I was around too many people who did, and eventually I started getting curious. It seemed like doing drugs was the thing to do. When I was at my girlfriend's apartment, her two cousins who used intravenous drugs were usually there too. They often shot up right in front of us. Sometimes they would leave a pack of dope just lying on the table.

One time I watched carefully what one of them did. When she left, I got a spoon, put cotton and water in it, measured it and cooked it. I had a lot of big veins in my arms, so I just stuck it into one of them. Most people start by skin popping — shooting drugs under the skin — until the muscles in their arms get too hard and then they start doing the intravenous stuff.

What did it feel like? It felt like I was going into another world and resting. I wasn't dead, but my mind was sure silent. The high took me way down, and I felt like I was in a kind of sleep.

During my last years of high school, I was going to school, using drugs and selling drugs all at the same time. Nobody ever referred me to any kind of help. Fooling my mother was no problem because she was totally ignorant about drugs. When people started telling her that her son was getting high, I don't think she wanted to believe them. And she didn't know how to help me get out of the mess I had gotten into when we moved to New York. Over the twenty-some years that I used drugs, I never went to a drug counselor or a special program or anything.

When I was about 19, another guy and I started working and selling together. The police had just caught the crew of drug dealers around the corner from our people, so we were on surveillance. When the police did their raid, they ran right into where we were stashing and selling. But when they arrested everybody, including me, I didn't have any drugs on me so I was only arrested for trespassing and being in a place I had no right to be in. I never got a drug record.

There was a lot of pressure to use, and I always thought I had to go along with the rest of the crowd. Almost everybody in my group was using long before I ever got started. I had older friends who had drug habits — nurses, bus drivers, civil service workers and city workers. I knew, because they came to me to buy their stuff. These people were holding down jobs and getting high at the same time.

I tried to get high only after work and on the weekends. Eventually I started making a lot of money with the drugs, and I didn't really need my job working in the post office.

I think a lot of the juniors and seniors in my high school were drug addicts, but you couldn't always tell. In those days, you could easily get yourself a shot in the morning before you went to work or school. That would keep you going for eight hours. When you went home, if you didn't already have your stuff you'd stop and get it. Then you'd go home and inject your afternoon shot. In the morning you'd start over again. Depending on how much stuff you were taking, if you didn't get a shot in the morning, you'd probably have trouble staying in school or on the job. You might be nauseated, trembling and full of chills.

I always had my stuff. I was never without it. I could afford it, because I was making so much money selling. I always had my regular deliveries, so I didn't have to go on the street and push. If I bought a $2 bag, I'd sell it for $20. Eventually the prices went up a lot. The dealers were holding back to raise the demand for drugs. A bag that I used to buy for $2 went up to $10.

Drug dealers usually don't keep their supplies in the place where they live. When they know they might get raided, they stay with their families. If the police knock on the door and see two or three kids and a pregnant lady in there, they'll probably go to the next apartment. Dealers often pay someone to store drugs in their apartment. That's how they survive. That stuff still goes on today, but most of the dealers are much younger now. They start sometimes as young as nine, and often they have guns. It's much more dangerous.

Actually I didn't sell most of my drugs in Manhattan. I had Caucasian customers who came down to Harlem from Connecticut. They picked me up in a car and took me to some drug users up there. All I had to do was get the drugs, they'd take me there, they'd sell them, they'd give me my money and bring me back to Harlem. What I sold for $2 in Harlem, I could sell for $30 in Connecticut. And if I opened a bag and made two bags out of it here, up there I could make three bags from one. The quality there was less than it was in Harlem.

I couldn't tell my mother that I had a lot of money hidden away in the apartment. I wanted to tell her, but I was afraid she would have me locked up. Even though people told her I was using, she didn't have any proof. Eventually in 1995, when I was no longer using, I told her that I used to get high. Now if I ever think about doing anything that is bad or wrong for me, I've promised to tell her. There wasn't really anything she could have done when I was a kid, but now I won't lie to her because I'm a grown man with children.

Nowadays, when I go to a party with my friends, I might have a drink. But I'm no longer searching for that same kind of high that I wanted when I was 20 years old. I don't want to drag myself down to a pattern I don't want to be in anymore. I've messed up a lot of things in the past, and now I'm choosing something else.

Although I was ignorant about drugs at first, I guess I survived the drug habit because I watched and learned some things. If I was going to use, I had to do it right. If I didn't care who did it with me or where I left the tools I used, that would have killed me. I had sense enough not to share a needle. There was always something inside me that really cared and had pride. I'm sure that came from my mother, who raised me to take care of myself and my body.

Many young teenage guys were using and coming down with hepatitis and other infections. Man, that's all I needed to know. Although I hung out with a bunch of guys and sold them drugs, I didn't get high with them. Back in the '60s and '70s, people would get together in a big room. One person would use the needle and maybe rinse it off with hot water and then pass it on to the next guy. But that doesn't take the blood particles out of the syringe. Eventually a whole lot of people in that group would end up being contaminated. Whatever one got, they all got.

Many of the white guys who came from the suburbs would stop by on Friday evenings. They'd usually go to one of the galleries around Harlem, where the people who ran the galleries supplied the needles. Often those customers who came only once a week would be really craving for the stuff. They might be sweating and having stomach cramps and throwing up. They wouldn't take the time to think about who had been in the place or that the needle might not be clean enough to use. They'd just want to get the syringe and needle and find a vein. Two or three weeks later they might have some kind of contamination.

I eventually started selling my drugs in those galleries, since every one who went there was looking for stuff, and I could sell easily and quickly. Many of the rich white kids from the suburbs went to the galleries since they couldn't go out on the streets to buy, because people would think they were the police or somebody might try to rob them.

A really well-known young man was robbed and murdered inside one of those galleries in a hotel on 117th Street. None of us knew who he was, even though he had been buying drugs from us for years. He had his own special room in that gallery. He came by often and bought a lot from us — thousands of dollars worth of stuff. He had a big, heavy habit, and he must have supplied other users too. Sometimes he'd come in on a Friday night and stay until late Sunday evening or Monday morning.

One morning I saw a lot of police kicking in the door across the hall. Someone told me a young white boy had been murdered there. The police couldn't find his wallet so they had to do a fingerprinting. When they found out who he was, man oh man, they had police in that place for months.

After that murder I decided it was time to move away. I had seen enough, and I had abused myself enough. I realized what dope using was all about. If you didn't get yourself out of it, it would kill you. I saw guys who had been handsome and smart and all that, and in six months time you couldn't believe that they could be that messed up.

There was one guy people called Claw. He had used so much dope that his hand was infected and swollen and heavy, and he had to put a sling around his neck to hold it up. People sometimes tested drugs before they took them to the streets, and lots of people gave him drugs to test. He had so many different chemicals in his system, his whole body was a mess. Eventually he had to have his arm cut off. It was terrible.

I was in my late 20s when I started trying to quit, and I really stopped using when I was in my 30s. The main thing that made me stop was that I knew this wasn't the life I wanted to live. I saw too many people who had a lot of stuff going for them, but when they got into drugs it changed their whole appearance and took everything they had worked for: their house, their car, their jewelry, their money in the bank, their health, sometimes their life. They lost it all.

Eventually the money I made in drugs was bad money, so I couldn't get rid of it the way I wanted. I couldn't put it in a bank, and I couldn't tell my mother I had it. If I let the wrong person know I had it and was stashing it, they would tell on me, or they'd try to get it from me.

One time I was arrested, but they couldn't find any drugs since I had them hidden away. When I was released, I took all the drugs I had and sold them. That was the last package I sold. Once I stopped dealing and was still using, the money went out real fast. Most people need to sell or steal to keep a habit like I had. But I didn't want to do it that way, stealing from my own people. Once you hurt your own family and friends, you don't have anyone to turn back to when you do try to clean up. I had younger brothers who never used and never knew I did.

Once I started doing bad things, I moved away from my family to an environment where there were people doing the same things I was doing. I couldn't introduce my brothers and their friends to that kind of stuff, or they'd end up doing the same kind of thing. After I started to clean up my habit, I could mix again with my brothers and the people in my neighborhood where my family was.

I stopped using for almost two weeks on my own. It was about that time when the methadone drug came out. I had a lot of friends who were using it, and it seemed like they were having a more normal lifestyle. I was really curious about it so I got on the wait list and eventually got into the methadone program.

At first they started me with 50 mg, but the stuff was really strong and I couldn't function properly. I was afraid if I kept using it I would be really high. The methadone was giving me almost the same feeling as heroin. I was told that when you stop using methadone, you have withdrawal pains just like with regular drugs. That felt like another trap; I was trading one drug for another. I really wanted to be straight off drugs.

I asked my counselor to make an appointment with my doctor. The next day I told the doctor that the stuff was killing me faster than dope. The methadone was taking over my body and my immune system. I wouldn't be able to fight off illnesses like colds, flu or pneumonia. This didn't seem better to me. So the doctor started bringing me down fast until I was at 5 mg. Then he gave me a little pill that was supposed to help flush the methadone out of my system.

Everybody told me I would hurt and ache and wouldn't be able to walk. I didn't care. I just didn't look back. I started doing all the exercises I could, I played sports, I stayed active, I meditated, I sweated out a lot of stuff, I got rid of the extra weight I didn't need. In two months, my body was in great shape again. I had my mind and body back under control. Even when I went past the same group of people where I had been getting high for years and years, I didn't have any interest in the drugs. I was clean.

To me, it seems the only way you can really be sure you're all right is if you're able to go back in your own environment again and not use. You can try to run away, but there's no place where you can hide from it. Drugs are everywhere. The only way you can beat it is to be right there where it is. And you can't get discouraged; just keep working at beating it. If you're a hundred miles away from the stuff, you haven't proven anything. If you're healed, you can be in the middle of the stuff and you won't want it. I'm in the middle of drug paradise, but that doesn't make me want to get high. I guess you could say that it's just plain willpower. I've never gone back to drugs since.

Although I was already a father when I was only seventeen and I had seven kids, fortunately, not one of my kids has ever been addicted to heroin. My first wife Luelle, who came from North Carolina, was a really wonderful woman, and she sure wanted our kids to have a good life. Unfortunately, she got sick with cancer and died when I was 27. I knew I had to do something about my children. My mother and my sisters said they would help raise them until I got my life straightened out.

After I was really finished with all the drug stuff, I began to realize all the things I had done to myself by being a user all those years. It wasn't long before I started swelling up, getting fevers and having to urinate and urinate. I got really tired and needed a lot of rest. I couldn't do the things I used to do, like play basketball.

One time I was really sick with a fever. My brother had to take me to the hospital, where they told me I had kidney failure. The doctors explained that all the drinking and drugs had caused my problem. I must have looked pretty bad, for my younger brother looked at me and said, "Are you gonna die?" And I said, "No, God's not ready to take me yet." I just didn't want to die; I realized I really wanted to live.

When I came out of the first surgery and learned I was going to have to be on dialysis, I couldn't believe it was happening to me. They kept telling me I had to take good care of myself or I wouldn't be able to live a healthy life and I might die. I felt terrible, really out of it. I'd never ever been very sick or hospitalized. I was used to a lot of activity in my life. I didn't want to be sitting around hooked up to a machine in a hospital all day, because I didn't think I could take it.

I didn't do what I needed to do for myself. I ate all the wrong food, gained weight and lost my strength, I got really depressed and snappy, and my self-esteem started going down. I had a pretty serious attitude problem. About four months into dialysis I got really badly infected, and I just stopped going. I finally got so sick that I started hallucinating and reliving many of the bad things that had happened to me before I was on dialysis.

Eventually I had to go back to the hospital again, this time in an ambulance. I was admitted to the hospital for three weeks, where I went back on dialysis. Finally things started getting better. So when I got out, I thought, "Well, now I can go off dialysis and be my old self again." I started playing sports and having fun. But it wasn't long before I was really sick again. So I went back to the hospital for the third time. There was a new staff, including a doctor who, I felt, didn't like me. It seemed they didn't want to accept me back in the dialysis unit again.

That's when I went to Bellevue. There was one nurse who was some kind of a nun. She would tell me things I didn't want to hear, and she would scold me out any time I missed a session or did something wrong. She made me mad because she made me feel like I was a little kid again. I didn't like it that she was right and I was wrong. But eventually I started realizing it was because she really cared for me and wanted to get the best medical treatment for me. She began to talk with me every day when I came in. It wasn't long before I started feeling better when I did the things she told me to do.

Of course, I had to change my lifestyle, and I couldn't do many of the things I had done. I had to eat well, get plenty of rest and sleep, and stay calm. Every time I got mad or went into a rage, it would make my blood pressure go up, and that made me much worse. My nurse kept trying to teach me to make myself strong and to have a good life. She even told me to focus on thinking that I was getting strong. She was a real professional.

Eventually I started liking her and calling her Sister. She was a very important person in my life because she talked straight to me, and she didn't make any excuses about things. She didn't try to keep from hurting my feelings, since she wanted me to know the way it was. If my feelings were hurt, well, I would get over it. But if I didn't do the right thing, I wouldn't.

Before long I started doing everything she told me to do because I could tell she was being really straight with me. Eventually Sister and I had a real understanding about stuff.

My other four nurses on the dialysis unit have been very special people in my life too. They laugh and joke with me, and they're always there for me. They're almost like my friends. My doctor is also very good to me. She explains the different kinds of dialysis to me, what an operation would be like, what would happen if I didn't do something, all the details. I always know what to expect. She also has the nurses call me if I don't show up for an appointment. I know she cares about me.

Another woman has been a special friend for me. She helped me get off drugs. She was always teaching me things that helped me get through life and through this dialysis. She taught me about how to live in the world, how to read and write well, how to sit and deal with people in a better way so I wouldn't have to be nervous and get a complex. She taught me that when I go out into the world, all I have to do is be myself and do the good things I've been taught and I'll get through life. Now she's moved to another city to be with her kids, and we've lost contact. But she'll be with me forever. I was lucky to have her, because she cared so much.

Of course, my mother has always been there for me, making sure I do the right things in life for myself and for other people. My parents, even though they weren't educated, always tried to do the best thing by their family. I think that helped me to be strong too. They certainly didn't know anything about drugs. I could have set the stuff right on the table in front of them, and they wouldn't have known what it was. They were so focused on surviving and taking care of us that they didn't know about the drug scene.

If I were to give advice to doctors and nurses, I'd tell them they should really try to listen to the patients and focus on helping them deal with depression and healing their minds. Maybe they could inspire them to do something positive. They shouldn't show their prejudices and dislikes. It makes people lose their confidence, and they can't get well. When you deal with sick people, you need to give them all you got so they can do what they have to do to get well.

Most of my doctors and nurses here at Bellevue have shown nothing but love for me. I'm healthy because of things they helped me to learn. Because of that, I am really much more able to take care of myself and be on my own.

Now I'm trying to do everything I'm supposed to do. I wake up every morning feeling good. I have a positive sense of spirit that carries me through the day and takes me through the night. If you have willpower and self-esteem, your body can fight off things much better, and you'll come back really strong.

The power of a single glance or an encouraging smile must never be underestimated.
— G. Richard Rieger

Although there are problems and setbacks from time to time, Charlie is clean and sober. His problems and defects have taught him lessons that he shares with others, and he has learned not to focus on the past with regret. Today he is a hopeful role model for other patients on his dialysis unit.

Charlie's story is especially impressive because of his candor and honesty. It is rare that drug users or dealers talk frankly about the things they have done. Often if we have troubled or dark histories, we may be ashamed and try to hide what has happened. That can lead to our remaining distressed, bitter and guilt-ridden. If, however, we learn from Charlie and choose to pull our past out of the shadows into the open, we may rediscover some of the lost parts of our selves and move forward.

Charlie's newly restored life demonstrates how important it is to choose to live in the present moment with a sense of gratitude and appreciation for the support we receive and the opportunities to change our tales of woe into stories of hope and healing.

BETTY

Tower of Awakening

*It was obvious that my parents did not want me to take on
a black identity. So I internalized the notion that there was something
wrong with black people, and I began to feel uncomfortable with them.
I had a strong sense that I didn't belong anywhere.* – Betty

Having grown up on a farm in the Midwest where there were very few
interactions with blacks — or other races for that matter — I can't begin
to claim to have a real understanding of the pain and suffering of racism.
But I know that the words "liberty and justice for all" are not accurate in
the white man's country of the United States, with its history of
discrimination, slavery and prejudice.

In my class at Nebraska Wesleyan University, there was a solitary
black student who was inconspicuous, unnoticed and "anonymous." I
don't recall his name and I barely remember him. I have no idea how he
survived such a cruel and lonely experience.

Trying to stand in the two worlds of white and non-white while
feeling unaccepted, unwanted and identity-less in either one of them

must fill one with confusion, anxiety, stress and sorrow. Perhaps it can be compared to what happens to refugees when they've lost their home, their country and their identity. Under such conditions life can feel overwhelming, hostile, defeating and meaningless.

My friend Mary Zepernick, with whom I had worked and been buddies for years, is one of the most fervent and courageous fighters I know in the battle against the crippling oppression of racism and sexism. As the U.S. President of the Women's International League for Peace and Freedom (WILPF), she fearlessly confronted these injustices with an awesome energy. Several years ago, Mary introduced me to Betty Burkes, a gifted, intelligent black woman living in Cape Cod, who became the WILPF president three years after Mary's term ended.

Betty

My life, of course, begins at the beginning. In fact, it began before the beginning, because who I am has a lot to do with where I came from. A great deal of history and experience came to fruition at my birth.

In the late 1930s, at my grandmother's insistence, my grandparents migrated to the North to flee the conditions of the South and to escape sharecropping. My dad was their only child born in the South, and he was sent North at an early age to be educated. But growing up in a small town, he experienced the essence of racism, discrimination and prejudice. He wasn't allowed to play sports, so he went to school in a neighboring town where he excelled.

Everybody knew my dad was the best player on the team, an athlete of Jackie Robinson's caliber. But when the recruiters came around, he wasn't selected because he was black. Somehow it never made him bitter or angry. He'd just grin out of the side of his mouth and say: "They're not bad. They just don't know any better." So I grew up believing that people could change if they were given appropriate information.

My dad was an incredibly moral, ethical human being, remarkable in many ways. As a child, I was aware of the power and respect he held in our community. He was a self-made man, but he didn't define himself racially.

My early years seemed exquisite. We lived in a home that housed my parents, my grandparents, my aunts and my uncles. My dad was the firstborn of eleven children, the beloved apple of my grandparents' eyes. Being the first of his children and the first grandchild, and being female in a matriarchal family structure, made everything feel truly wonderful for me.

Because my grandfather worked for the brick mill, our family home was set within a circle of company houses in a community of multicultural families: Poles, Italians, Germans, English and African-Americans. Everyone who lived on the circle worked for the plant. They shared the same poverty and injustices. When there was conflict, my parents and other adults around me blamed it on economics and character problems. Of course, it was also racism, but at the time our sensibilities didn't pick up on that.

My dad was away at the War during my early years, so my uncles and aunts played a very important role for me. A new reckoning came when I was five and my parents and their children split off from the rest of the family. This was perceived as a step up for them. Although my parents were ecstatic about moving into their own home, I was devastated to have my source of security removed and to move into a single-family house with just my dad and mom. It was an enormous loss that I never totally recovered from and that no one ever acknowledged.

Still, life was pretty good for me as I started elementary school. During my first year school felt great, and I had a strong sense of myself. There was no doubt that I was good, brilliant, beautiful, loved and perfect! Everybody said so. After all I was the first!

When I was in the third grade, the school planned an open house for parents. Our class was to perform a square dance, and I expected to dance. But my teacher told me I couldn't dance "because little brown girls didn't dance with white boys." It was crushing news to learn that there was something wrong with me because I was "brown" and therefore unable to participate in a public event that my mom and dad would attend. I was an innocent nine-year-old. That event shut me down, and I began to check out.

From then on, I wasn't quite myself, and things started getting difficult. There were enormous expectations from my family that I, the beloved firstborn, would excel at any cost. I was the child who would move the whole family forward. Therefore, I performed well. I was in the national honors society. I was head librarian and a majorette. I acted in plays and played in the band. I forced the school system to let me in, but at a huge price to myself.

In many ways my family raised me apart from the black community. My family was among the shakers and movers at a black church. But I didn't go to parties and I didn't date. Although there were other black kids in my school, I never had much to do with them. Occasionally they came over to my house, but that was closely monitored, and I was never alone with them. I don't recall visits or play dates at their homes. My parents often held up images of black girls that they didn't want me to be. Very early on, I got the message that I was not like them. I was to be different and better.

In the summer, I was sent away to camp with white girls, or we went on a family trip. My dad was very intentional about giving me a bigger experience. He didn't want me to get the impression that my future was limited to where I grew up. There was never a question about going to college; I always knew I would.

It was obvious that my parents did not want me to take on a black identity. So I internalized the notion that there was something wrong with black people, and I began to feel uncomfortable with them and confused about race. I must have felt a bit schizophrenic that the person in my skin was not like people in other skins of the same color. My best friend was a white girl. My hopes and dreams were not inspired by anyone in the local community, black or white.

Since the beginning, my identity has been non-racial. I never identified myself as a black or white girl, and I was never in a racial group. It was a peculiar kind of upbringing — living among black people but not feeling like one of them. I had a strong sense that I didn't belong anywhere.

My dad was interested in many things and especially in Africa. Often he invited African students from the college over to our house for the holidays. I developed an interest in Africa and the larger world; I knew that someday my escape would be into that world. I couldn't wait to get out of Malvern, Ohio.

During my sophomore year of high school, I had an incredible crush on an Italian boy. We walked together to school and flirted a lot. My mother started getting nasty phone calls: "You tell your 'nigger' daughter to stay away from white boys." In his junior year he went away. I assumed that decision had something to do with our friendship.

In my senior year, I finally felt the full force of the shaming effects of racism. I had the highest grades and was voted the girl most-likely-to-succeed in my class. But I didn't receive the scholastic honors I earned. At the ceremony where an award for the girl with the highest grade point average was presented, I knew my name would be called. But it was awarded to the girl who had been my best friend, not to me. I was shocked. It reminded me of the third grade incident: "Little brown girls don't dance with white boys."

After that I started acting out and going with C. L., a black guy who was ten years older than I was. We rode around in a car together, but we never did anything "wrong." I was too much of a prude. When I invited C. L. to the senior prom, he didn't arrive to escort me. My mother asked my uncle to drive me to the prom. I remember sitting at the dinner table trying to eat and then going to the bathroom where I stayed until I was collected. That was another reckoning moment for me.

My life seemed dreadful after that horrible night. I felt deeply humiliated and wanted to die. My dad was totally confused by my behavior. He didn't know what to do with his beloved daughter who had always been very reasonable.

Not long after the disastrous prom, I packed up and moved to Columbus, Ohio, where my dad had managed to get me a summer job working for the state. That fall I began attending Ohio State University, so I didn't go home until Christmas. And I've never returned to the high school or any event associated with it.

In Malvern, I felt people regarded me as eccentric, as someone who never quite fit in and just didn't add up. I was always the odd one out. I didn't belong to the black or white community; I didn't belong anywhere. I felt disconnected. I was somewhere in a crack.

Years later after I left the States to serve in the Peace Corps, my parents wanted me to return to Malvern and be acknowledged for the person I had become. They would shake their heads: "It's a shame you don't visit some of the people who were part of your life." But I felt there was nothing for me to go back to, and I didn't feel any attachment to the people who had had a part in shaping my life.

My dad and mom always wanted me to be normal, even though they raised me to be different. They couldn't understand why I wasn't like everybody else. Why did I have to travel half way around the world? Why did I have to live in Europe for fifteen years? Why can't Betty Jean be like . . .? It was bizarre that they had those kinds of expectations when all the messages they'd given me were contrary to that.

Even when I went away to college, I was still a stranger to myself. I had not fully recovered from the conflicting and shaming events that had happened to me. I functioned and appeared normal most of the time, but I wasn't totally there and college life seemed overwhelming to me. One year I was a really "good girl" — a dorm counselor — and the next year I was a "bad girl" — threatened with being thrown out of the dormitory because I refused to play by the rules. I thought they were unfair, and I didn't feel obliged to abide by rules that I had no say in establishing.

Many black students were members of fraternities and sororities, which was not at all my interest. In my mind there was something wrong with institutions that were isolated and not integrated.

When I first went to Columbus, I met Mike, my first real black boyfriend. His family was Catholic and of a different kind of culture than the black people in my hometown. His parents were urban and educated, and he introduced me to a black world that I hadn't known before. It was my first encounter with the black bourgeoisie.

Then I met some black intellectuals, including Walter from Los Angeles, whose father was a lawyer. We spoke a similar language of rebellion and soon became very involved with each other. He enjoyed a level of comfort within the black community that I didn't have. He seemed brilliant and comfortable in any circle of people.

During college I never had a best girlfriend who was black. I thought maybe I talked differently or people could sense something about me that was scary. Walter said it was the language I used and there was something about the way I had been acculturated that put black people off. I was like a "black duckling."

After four years of a liberal arts education, I graduated with a degree in political science and a specialty in African affairs. But I didn't have a clue about what I was going to do with my life. Then one day as I was walking through the student union, I saw a sign that the last Peace Corps exams were to be given that day. On a whim, I took the exam, passed it, and went to Peace Corps training. As a new volunteer, I was off to Eritrea to teach history, science and English as a second language.

After I finished my Peace Corps contract, I began a new chapter in my life. I took a job teaching in a predominately black elementary school in Los Angeles. I went into therapy and started studying early childhood education at UCLA. I delved into my work with my therapist. He was male and black. That seemed bizarre to me at the time; I had never been in a professional relationship with a black man. But I persevered on faith. I soon discovered that the condition of my "integrated self" was not very intact after all. The only thing that held me together was sheer stubbornness.

Working with the therapist was one of the first steps in my healing process. When I stopped seeing him three years later, I thought I was finished. But it was just the beginning of my journey. Little by little I started getting glimpses of myself and my various roles, including how I related to my family, how I denied my race, how I had internalized race and class consciousness, and how that kept me from relating to blacks who were not in my class. My life didn't look very different, but it felt different. Most people probably didn't even notice. For the first time, I was developing a relationship with myself.

My move to Berkeley was the next major piece of my life. I became involved with a wonderful group of women with whom I did team-teaching at a middle school. One of them was Mary, a black woman who became a very good friend — my first close relationship with a black woman.

The team teaching was the best job I ever had because it was primarily about community and a commitment to integration. The women were skilled and willing to struggle with issues of race and class in order to provide both black and white children the best education there was. It was my first head-on collision with the notion of black power.

During my college years I had been involved peripherally with a YWCA program testing housing discrimination. I was curious and aware of the sit-ins and bus rides taking place in the South at the time. But I was too confused and divided in myself to be deeply involved.

When I moved to Berkeley in the late '60s, it was a time of school desegregation and busing. In our school district, teams of black educators were in charge of teaching black history. There were meetings everywhere as we tried to address centuries of racism and injustice. Everyone agreed the best way was through education. The challenge we saw was to create a safe place for children to learn about each other and to bridge and appreciate cultural differences that the wounds of race and class had impeded.

That put my history and me right in the middle of the debates. I did not come from a place of anger at whites; my oppression had not been solely linked to white people. Four years of therapy had helped me get clear about some of the root causes of my oppression, and race wasn't the only factor. I didn't need to discharge personal frustration and distress in the workplace. In the racially charged city of Berkeley, which was both torn and deeply committed to racial justice, there were many challenges. Our teaching team was committed to facilitating community and to making the Berkeley busing experiment a success.

The next summer I traveled to Africa where I met Beach, a Peace Corps volunteer. We hit it off right away. When he finished his assignment, he joined me in Berkeley. He was a liberated young man who touched a part of me that hungered for freedom from the struggles and politics of race and gender that Berkeley came to represent. He offered me a way out and I took it.

Because of our beliefs around the Vietnam War, Beach and I decided to leave the United States in 1971. We gave most of our worldly possessions away and hitchhiked across the country. On our way we stopped to see my parents in Ohio. They were mortified that I, a professional woman, was heading off to Europe with a white guy and a backpack.

As it turned out, deciding to leave the United States was a turning point in my pursuit of wholeness and health. In London, Beach began studying astrology, and I took an art course in clay. Eventually he returned to the States, but I stayed because I was deeply involved in my artwork. Beach had shown me a different perspective on living that helped give me permission to step outside the expected into a reality of my own choosing. He served as a bridge to the next chapter of my life.

An important aspect of my healing came through my introduction to clay by a remarkable man and teacher. Alan was a rigorous, spiritual person whose message to me was: "I'll go with you on this journey of self-exploration if you commit to it." He opened his life, the world of art, his family, friends, home and beauty to me. He became my mentor and guide. He held up a mirror that enabled me to see my own transformation taking place.

Alan didn't care whether I was white, black or purple as long as I produced a beautiful pot with integrity. He was the first person who invited me to clarify my values and purpose in life. He challenged me to challenge myself. He didn't ask, "Who are you?" Rather, in our work he continuously pushed me to ask myself that question. Creating sculptures and pots was the process, and clay was the material for exploring those questions.

During the Second World War, Alan had suffered a spinal injury. But he had no time for self-pity; he willed himself to walk and had a miraculous recovery. Although Alan was compassionate and cared about personal injuries, he was also deeply interested in pushing himself and his students beyond emotional and physical limitations. He was intensely committed to the spiritual journey of the creative self. Alan stated his philosophy in two ways: (1) Acknowledging that we are all damaged in the pursuit of living, let's get on with the work we've chosen to do, and (2) Lay down your victim and pick up your potential.

Certainly Alan's life was a departure from anything I had known. With his guidance, I gained a deeper awareness of the natural world, and I began to experience the artist side of me — the person who couldn't draw an acceptable picture in grade school. My life began to have direction, and there was a strong sense of being on a quest within myself and within my cultural heritage.

While attending a music workshop in the fall of 1973, I met Paul, a white, sophisticated jazz musician. Although I was cautious, he was persistent. I was flattered and amused by his attention, but when I met Paul I wasn't looking for someone to fill my missing parts. I had been in too many consuming relationships with men, and I was feeling more confident and comfortable with my independence. My yoga, dance and sculpting activities were centering and affirming, and I was beginning to experience a quality of wholeness in my living. After a year of dating, we decided to live together.

Going into therapy, leaving the U.S., having a community of like-minded friends and discovering my creative potential were all significant landmarks on my road toward health and wholeness. They were also a preparation for the birth and parenting of my daughter.

Emily was born in England in 1978. Her premature birth and a complicated illness afterwards put a strain on Paul and me. However, after I had fully recovered, we worked hard at trying to restore some stability to our relationship.

Emily was the focus and center of my life. Her wellbeing and development became my work, and being her mom became my identity. I loved her unconditionally. Gradually, I noticed the astonishing fact that loving Emily was an act of self-love. Loving myself by loving her served as a powerful healing potion.

Nurturing and caring for Emily have been the most affirming and self-fulfilling work I've ever done. Her developmental stages have been accompanied by my own development. The partnership that has emerged between us has challenged and stimulated my growth and development as well as hers. When she has prospered and grown, so have I. For me, parenting has been an opportunity to be intentional about the quest for my true self.

Eventually Paul and I decided we had to move back to the States. Emily was about to start school, and I was concerned about the race and class issues. I wasn't as confident about negotiating those oppressions in England as well as I could in the U.S. If we remained in London, we knew we would probably have to choose a private school for Emily. But we both supported public education and wanted her to have that experience. To take her out of the state schools would have been a compromise for us. So we left England and moved to Cape Cod.

Returning to the U.S. was the completion of a cycle for me. I was right back where I had started, reentering a system and a country that had wounded me critically in the past. But much about me had changed, and the next years would both test and strengthen those changes.

One of the first problems that confronted us on Cape Cod was racism: the issue I had fled fifteen years earlier. Emily was six when we returned to the States and enrolled her in the first grade at the local elementary school. Not long after school started, she was called a "dirty nigger" by a little girl on the school bus. She was hurt and confused.

Right then I realized that the work I'd left undone had been patiently waiting for my return. This time I was able to find my voice as Emily's ally and fellow traveler on our journey. I could embrace this opportunity to resist racism for both of us. When I had been her age, I did not have an advocate, nor could I be my own. But I could be Emily's. By becoming Emily's mother, I became a mother to myself.

Immediately I called the school: "We need to talk. I'm not worried about Emily; I can take care of her. But any little girl who says such a thing to my daughter must be in a lot of pain. How can we help? Let's have a meeting with her parents to see what we can do to make this community a safe place for everybody."

That was the beginning of my pro-active life locally. Shortly after the discussion with the school principal, I realized I was reliving my own history. Only this time I was the adult.

A year later I opened a Montessori School to recreate the school Emily had attended in London. The goals of the school were to build community and to empower children. I knew the only way we change the world is by changing the values and attitudes of people. I hoped my work at the school would have a positive impact on the community and make a difference in a small way — like dropping a pebble in a pond.

About a year after I opened the school, Mary Zepernick, who later became the U.S. President of the Women's International League for Peace and Freedom (WILPF), asked if the kids at my school would do artwork on peace for children's T-shirts. Before long I was attending WILPF meetings and feeling the benefits of the supportive community of the members who were educating people and confronting oppression. I learned from them that a caring and supportive community is key to transforming and healing society and ourselves.

Eventually, Mary invited me to attend a Leadership Institute training in Seattle. There, around a big table, participants told their stories. As I listened, I realized that although the details were different, the stories were very similar. I learned that racism is an intentional tactic of the white patriarchal system that dominates the affairs of much of the world. Racism, as a tool of capitalism, has been used in most countries to divide and conquer for the purposes and benefits of capitalism.

Understanding the politics of racism has been a powerful experience for me. Now I know that we must act politically, not just emotionally, to eradicate racism. I can go into schools and teach multi-cultural education, but WILPF taught me that if I don't make the connections between racism and politics, then I'm not helping to create change for a better world. That launched my political life and my liberation.

My greatest teacher and healer has been my daughter Emily. I realize that when I gave birth to her, I gave birth to myself. Her beginning was also my beginning. Loving her, and therefore loving myself, has presented me openings to my own recovery. Accompanying Emily through the natural process of discovering her world, I was able to reclaim mine. Parenting Emily has provided me opportunities to struggle and grow. Through our special relationship, I have been able to pursue my journey toward liberation and wholeness. For me, that journey has been challenging and worth traveling.

Suffering and the timeless dark nights of the soul are a necessary, maybe unavoidable, prelude to the ultimate odyssey — our journey within.

— Susan Skog

Betty, like many other victims of prejudice and discrimination, was all too familiar with the dark nights of the soul — the chilling feelings of isolation, of no true identity, of not belonging. The conflicting messages Betty received about her race from her parents and society, coupled with the discrimination she experienced as she grew up, caused her to be uncomfortable in her own skin and scarred her deeply, making her feel almost powerless.

Betty's healing process has been complicated and has taken place over several decades with much assistance from supportive people, especially from a disabled man who didn't believe in wallowing in problems. He challenged Betty to reach deep inside her soul and reclaim her genuine self.

Ironically, Betty's greatest growth took place when she witnessed the racism her daughter experienced. While helping her child walk through the maze of racism and bigotry, Betty "rebirthed" herself, matured and finally felt healed enough to be an advocate for herself and others.

Like Betty, we can choose to redeem parts of ourselves that may have been destroyed by societal judgments and values. Little by little, we may become more open to our potential and reclaim our authentic selves. Such a healing odyssey may uncover skills and talents that have always been rooted deep within us. Ultimately we too may claim our capacity to create a worthy and wholesome life for ourselves, our families and our communities.

GOLDY

Tower of Meaning

*Now I try to think about what I have and how I can learn
from this experience of dying and use those learnings in the time left.
I no longer say, "A year ago I was doing this."
That's one of the blessings of accepting my dying.* – Goldy

*Those 18 months were the greatest sharing experiences we ever had
with Mom. There wasn't anything that went unsaid, and every nook
and cranny were explored. I felt we were on sacred ground.* – Andy

Goldy was one of my dearest friends. We dreamed of one day opening
an alternative to a retirement or nursing home, where we would live
together with our friends, share resources and take care of each other as
we graciously grew older. We planned to have fun, travel, good food
and an enormous porch full of rocking chairs. But we never had a chance
to see our dream fulfilled. Before we reached a ripe old age, Goldy died
from an aggressive cancer, adenocarcinoma of the uterus, ovaries and
cervix that metastasized to her lungs and liver.

We first met in New York City when we both were preparing to work overseas: Goldy in West Africa and I in the slums of Karachi, Pakistan. Goldy's cheeks always seemed ablaze with rosy health, her eyes sparkled with a *joie de vivre,* and her energy was awesome. Over the years, our friendship deepened. Whenever I moved to a new location, a package of daffodil bulbs would arrive for my newest garden. Today there are lots of daffodils multiplying around the country in her honor.

On one of her visits, we opened a giant pink grapefruit for breakfast and found two seeds with long green roots. Since the seeds seemed to be screaming for a chance to live, we planted them in a pot. Eventually two rather scrawny grapefruit trees emerged. Although moving from place to place and living in my overheated Manhattan apartment has not been easy for them, the trees continue to have spurts of growth. Shortly after Goldy died, they produced about a dozen shiny new leaves, affirming life just like her!

From the onset of her illness, Goldy spoke openly about her imminent death. Like the grapefruit seeds, her story screamed to be told, to be alive. As my pal drew nearer to death, we agreed her story would be included in this book.

Goldy

During an unusually harsh winter in Philadelphia, I started feeling exhausted and short of breath. Looking back now to when I first learned about my cancer, I remember the terrible snowstorms we had that year. I felt so tired and thought either I was really slowing down or the weather was getting to me. When my sister and I went for walks, she walked faster than I could, which was unusual. Then my belt got really tight, and I wondered if middle-age spread was creeping up on me. Although I was rarely sick, I knew it was time for me to check in with a doctor. As she examined me, I told her, "I think I must have cancer." The doctor seemed concerned too because she immediately scheduled many tests for me.

On April Fools' Day, I could barely breathe and had difficulty getting dressed, so I called my doctor. She had just received the results of my tests. "I want you to check into the hospital right away," she said. In some ways I felt relieved, but when I learned it was on the cancer floor, my heart sank. The first two nights in the hospital I watched the sun go down and I watched it come up. I was so scared that I was dying that I couldn't sleep. One night I actually planned my funeral. I kept wondering how I, a medical person, didn't know earlier that there was something wrong with me.

From then on, life changed drastically for me. The diagnosis was frightening: Stage Four adenocarcinoma in my uterus, which had already metastasized in my lungs and liver. The rapidly growing cancer was spreading throughout my body. My prognosis: three to six months. To slow down the cancer, I immediately underwent radical chemotherapy treatments, which nearly shut down my kidneys and made me violently ill and extremely depressed.

All my life I've been an independent, highly responsible woman. I've lived alone in my own home. The unknown is nearly impossible for me to deal with. So I was adamant about getting information and the real picture about my situation. When the doctors asked my sons to step into the hall to talk about my situation, I was absolutely incensed. I got furious if they didn't include me in discussing information about my diagnosis or treatments. It was months before they were able to talk really straight to me.

I appreciate that they never lied to me or said they could cure me. Rather, they told me they could control my symptoms. Although part of me wanted the doctors to be gentle, because the truth was tough and often devastating to hear, I still preferred getting all the information. Yet I have to admit it was a shock when I first heard about the seriousness of my cancer.

When the home nurse came to my apartment, I asked her to tell me what it would be like to die. I wanted to know. I needed to know. I wanted information so I could do realistic planning for the future and for my death. She told me in great detail what the process might be. I found myself saying, "I think I can manage that; I think I can handle that pain." It was frightening to hear and it made me cry, but it was a gift for me to know. All my life I've been a person who wanted to know everything, to prepare in advance, to practice, so I would be ready for whatever happened. That certainly applied to facing my death.

I expected to be involved in decision making about my treatment, and I had definite ideas about what I did or didn't want for myself. My children are grown up, and I didn't need my body to be kept alive at all costs. I was looking for quality of life. Those were my ground rules.

I also wanted to learn about the impact of the drugs I was supposed to take to control some of the side effects of chemotherapy, such as nausea and diarrhea. I live alone, so I had to know if the drugs would make me be off balance. I wanted to be alert, to be able to remember things, to make judgments, to be somewhat in control, and to be as mentally clear and physically stable as possible. Most doctors aren't used to patients being so involved and aware of their situation.

There have been some positive effects of my illness too. I'm now able to tell doctors what I don't want. I don't care if something is "their thing" or if I hurt their feelings. I've even learned to say "no" to them. After all, this is my life and my death!

It's taken a long time for my family to talk openly about my death. They're probably more in denial about this than I am. It was almost humorous when one of my sisters said to me, "After your treatments are over, you'll be fine and you can start dating." My sons, of course, want me to live a long time and I'd love to do that, but I won't. And I couldn't keep up an illusion or a front of wellness for everyone. It was too exhausting. In fact, it took the living right out of me. That's not the way I want to live the remainder of my life. I have to be real with my family, my friends, with everyone.

When I first started with chemotherapy I was very sick, tired and weak. Although I love to cook and enjoy food immensely, I really couldn't eat, especially the hospital food. I'd look at it, and it looked terrible. I love to smell thyme, garlic, onions, lavender and rosemary. "If I could just have some of those spices around me," I thought, "I might be able to eat the bland food on the hospital tray." A friend brought me little bags of fresh spices, so I could open up those bags and smell real garlic or rosemary whenever I wanted. That helped, and I could eat that boring food just remembering how good things tasted and how good they might be again.

Chemotherapy was never easy for me. When I started, I felt really cold and nauseated. Joy helped me prepare and plan for those sessions with some special imagery techniques. During the treatments, I'd imagine something pleasant for me, like being in my own comfortable apartment with the smell of the garden outside and the sunshine flowing through the windows. Or I would take a favorite picture book to look at. We also discovered that if I took herbs with me in a plastic bag, such as fresh rosemary or lavender, even garlic, to smell during the treatment, I was able to relax. Sometimes I even slept during the treatment, and usually I didn't get sick afterwards.

One day I took a very funny book that made me laugh out loud. Before long some of the patients asked me about it. So I started to connect with them, which was good for me and for them. This gave me a tiny measure of control over the chemotherapy.

After I got home from my first hospitalization, I had to learn how to live alone with some of my disabilities, like not being able to walk well, not being able to feel or pick up things with my hands. The staff at the hospital and the hospice told me what I needed for my apartment: guard rails, a hospital bed and an easy chair that could assist me in getting up. When I thought about getting a chair, I wanted to choose something that was beautiful since I respond so positively to things that look, smell and taste good. I continue to surround myself with things of beauty that will help me heal. Just because I'm ill and dying, I don't have to settle for ugly things. I can still have furniture that is comfortable and beautiful.

I also had to plan how I would get shopping and cooking done and my place cleaned. These were major issues for me, because initially I had a hard time admitting that I was sick. It was like learning how to live another way, how to manage my body and how to exercise in a manner that wouldn't be harmful to me but would make me strong again after chemotherapy.

For me, it was important to be as independent as possible for as long as possible. My family and friends helped make that a reality. One son talked with doctors and gave information to the family, so I didn't have to do that and everyone got the same message. Another son dealt with important logistics such as social security, banking and Medicare. My third son made sure I was connected to the world through machines that didn't require a lot of strength, because we lived in different places around the country. He got us linked together with up-to-date communication technology.

My sisters helped me get clothes that are comfortable, warm and washable and very suitable for the new life I lead at home, in the hospital and in doctors' offices. I had to adjust to not being a professional woman who went to work and was always dressed up.

One of my sisters said, "You've always done things for others. Now let others do things for you." That wasn't easy because I've always been extremely independent. However, my energy and thinking abilities definitely started getting depleted when I was on chemotherapy, and I had to have help. I was really grateful when a friend volunteered to become a point person. She matched up what I needed with people who offered to do something for me. Some people brought books and read to me — whatever I wanted. Others brought food and visited with me, if I felt in the mood to do that. Someone took me to get my driver's license renewed.

There are many things family and friends can do to help sick or dying people, such as bringing food, following up with social security and taxes, getting medicines, putting money into and getting it from the bank, making sure a will is done properly, helping plan for funeral and burial arrangements, and assisting with financial planning.

In many ways I feel fortunate that I didn't have a massive heart attack or suddenly die in a car or airplane crash. I've had the gift of time so I could do things I still needed and wanted to do. I joined a mind-body seminar, which helped my healing process. It made such a difference for me to be with seventeen people who were doing the same exercises, relaxation and breathing techniques with me. It was such a non-judgmental group: They didn't tell you to buck up or pull up your socks. By the way, when people say those things, it's such a downer. No one in the group ever made comparisons, and they'd cheer you if you looked good with a new hat or a wig or if something special happened. I learned a lot from these people who were also facing death. They helped me tune into living with the reality of my pending death. It didn't cure me, but it was really healing.

Another special thing was taking a trip with family to Europe. When I first knew I was terminally ill, I started counting up the things I couldn't do anymore: I couldn't go to work, I couldn't swim, I couldn't garden, I couldn't travel. I couldn't do things that I loved. My son and his wife invited me to go to Italy with them, and we were able to work around the schedule for my chemo treatments. The minute I got on that airplane, I knew I was no longer a patient. It didn't matter that I was in a wheelchair. I was just another person — not a cancer patient — among people who didn't know I was sick or dying. Although it probably won't last forever, it put things in perspective, and it was wonderful.

Now I'm learning how to modify things that I always enjoyed and still want to do. For example, I love to garden, but I can't do that anymore. My family got one large container and put a few plants together in it, making it easy for me to care for them. So I have a manageable, small garden in my apartment. Also music is very important to me. I used to accompany professional singers on the piano. These days when I listen to classical music, I try to imagine that I am playing it, and I can almost feel my fingers on the keyboard. When I can't sleep at night, I listen to my music, especially Handel's "Water Music." It makes me feel peaceful, like I'm sailing on top of the waves.

Living alone with cancer in my own home, I realized I wasn't getting much physical touch. It's important for me to have eye-to-eye contact and to be touched by people. Being terminally ill helped me lose some of my inhibitions. I wanted my friends and family to sit on my bed and hold my hand, so I just told them to do that. I used to think massages were a luxury, but I don't think that way anymore. A person doesn't have to be a highly trained masseuse to help me. When someone just gently stretches out my stiff feet or fingers after a chemo treatment, it helps me get a night's sleep. One of my sons gave me a Christmas present of seven massages. That was glorious!

My illness has made me aware of how important it is to get issues and unfinished business out in the open — right now. I need to talk with my sons more and help them come to terms with my illness and with my impending death. They have such different personalities. It's been amazing to see how they deal with my illness and how this has changed them. I've seen them come alive and open up more to life and relationships.

At my church, the minister and I had been estranged from each other for some time. When he first came to the hospital, I wasn't sure I could trust him with my spiritual journey. But as we saw each other, I realized he had many gifts that could be useful to me. I needed to let the past die and move forward. As soon as I was willing to do that, he really was able to help me.

There was also some unfinished business with my mother. We had become quite distant from each other after my father's death. When I got sick, we both felt devastated. Since she is unable to travel, we thought we might never have the chance to see each other again or to resolve our problems. I decided to make the effort to reach out to my mother across the miles by phone. She reached right back to me by calling me every day. Since then we have been able to work through many things and have been able to forgive each other. We have built a new and wonderful relationship. I would say that's been one of the greatest miracles of my illness. When I was in remission and was well enough to fly on an airplane, I went to Iowa to see her. That visit was a tremendously healing experience for both of us. For the first time I see my mother as a real person and a real friend. We can interact as we really are with no masks or pretenses. Perhaps my mother is able to be more fully human knowing that she has been forgiven and that I really need her. Maybe she feels that she's the strong one now who can care for me. In a way my illness has become a gift for us, and we have healed each other.

Recently I saw my ex-husband. When he came to see me, I had been feeling sorry for myself that I didn't have a husband to take care of me. In fact I was really angry that he wasn't there for me "in sickness and in health." During our visit we had some serious and funny moments. It was truly a heartfelt conversation, for there were many things that hadn't been settled, and we still have our three sons in common. There was no feeling of victory for either of us, but rather a settling of the issues and an acknowledgment that the right decisions had been made. What had been had been. I was able to say what I needed to: that I hoped he would have a good relationship with each of the sons, especially after I'm gone. I want the boys to feel comfortable with their father and not be angry with him. So there was forgiveness and healing for both of us.

Other people with whom I've had arguments or conflicts in the past have met with me, and we too have dealt with our unfinished business. All of this has helped me forgive the past and move forward.

I believe it's critical to talk about whatever is on your mind and to do it before you're in the last stages of dying when it's really too late. I tell people not to wait until they're on their deathbed. If there is healing that still needs to be done in a person's life, one should go for it — right now. It doesn't have to be a perfect process either. Just making the effort helps a person to focus on the important things and can be healing.

People with whom I've had accomplishments have also stayed in touch with me. They helped me remember and re-create our stories, our successes. Some of my former work colleagues told me that I was still a part of their team; they even asked me to help them on a professional presentation. It was so affirming that they didn't write me off or make me feel like I was a drag on the process. Such a gift for me.

I've been deeply touched by people who have never discussed my spiritual life with me but who have told me I'm on their prayer lists. That's been very moving and supportive, and quite a revelation for me. Hearing these things has made me feel very humble and cared for.

One of the most difficult things for me about my illness and dying has been that I had always been such a high-energy person. I don't have much energy anymore. So I have had to learn how to set limits — especially related to responding to people who aren't positive. When I started doing that, I felt more in charge of controlling negative energy, and I truly moved into a healing process. Little by little I've started giving up people and things I need to let go of, and I feel much lighter, especially emotionally.

Looking back, I sometimes wonder how I was able to carry all of that in the past. Knowing and accepting that I'm tired and sick has been good for me. Now I just take a rest whenever I need it. I made a decision that I didn't need to take "uppers" or to mask things with chemicals. I want to be real about how I feel and know what's happening as much as possible.

Until recently I kept going back and forth thinking about the person I used to be and comparing that with my sick self. I've been able to quit doing that, and I've stopped counting my losses. Now I try to think about what I have and how I can learn from this experience of dying and use those learnings in the time left. I no longer say, "A year ago I was doing this." That's one of the blessings of accepting my dying; I have stopped comparing myself to who and what I was. I've adjusted to who I am now and am happy with that.

All of these things — the imagery, the meditation, making peace with everyone, finishing any unfinished business, accepting who and what I am — have helped me prepare for my death. I'm a little nervous about the deterioration of my body, the pain I might feel, the lack of control at the end, the sheer exhaustion of breathing, all of those things. But I think I'm ready to die. In fact, I'm kind of looking forward to it.

Andy

Mom was always the healthy one who looked after everyone. When the doctors told us she had six to nine months to live, maybe longer, and the treatments would start immediately and would be tough, it seemed very frightening. Mom always was totally self-sufficient, but that was no longer true. As her son I wanted to take control, but I felt almost helpless. I didn't know how to take care of my mother, especially since I lived a hundred miles away.

For the next eighteen months our family and friends rallied around Mom trying to make her as comfortable and relaxed as possible. We were constantly aware that there was a deadline out there and didn't know when she would be called.

My brothers and I wanted Mom to be the happiest person she could be in whatever time was left. In many ways her illness provided us a chance to give something back to her. We tried to figure out how to lovingly care for her so she could have some new experiences, do what she wanted to do and focus on herself — not on the trivial stuff.

We immediately set up her apartment so she could be in control for as long as possible. We made sure the hospice and home health care were available for her.

Mom was as worried about preparing us for her death as we were about her dying. When she talked with us, she acknowledged straightforwardly that she was dying. She told us the cancer would not go away, we would do some things to fight it, but we were not going to do extraordinary things — she had her limits. She had a living will, and her sister was going to execute it. When things got really rough, she didn't want to put up with a lot of pain. And we were going to have fun between now and whenever "that time" came. By setting up those guidelines she helped us.

It was amazing how Mom started blossoming after she knew she was dying. She went from being a person who always gave to others to being a person who could also graciously receive. Soon her whole demeanor was different: She was much more open and personal and no longer talked about frivolous things. She was very clear on how she wanted to spend her last days on earth: take no bullshit, spend time only with people she wanted to, talk about things she wanted to and do only meaningful things. That helped us focus on what was important in our lives.

Emily and I had been married for almost a year when Mom was first diagnosed. Her situation put us into a whole different mode in our relationship and helped us get clarity on what we wanted. We no longer had time for trivial stuff. We began looking at our spirituality and what we needed to sustain ourselves.

Those eighteen months were the greatest sharing experiences we ever had. I was able to talk with Mom about things that were really important to me, and she seemed to do the same. There wasn't anything that went unsaid, and every nook and cranny were explored. We were on sacred ground.

During that time, I went through some major changes. I realized I didn't have to stay in the job I didn't like. My mother had a ton of faith in me. So I left a job at Morgan Stanley, which most people would die for, and walked into an unfinished building downtown with eighteen people, an idea and some money in the bank. About the same time, both my younger and older brothers made changes in their work. Mom helped us learn that taking a risk is trying what you want and not being afraid to do it. She'd say: "Love what you do. If you don't, do what you need to do to find out what you want to do." Her pending death helped us improve our lives.

We tried to do special things with Mom before she died. Emily and I took her to Italy for a week, where we celebrated her birthday. Just before her death, the family gathered for Thanksgiving at her apartment and cooked a big meal. Mom always enjoyed good food. She wanted to taste everything, even though she knew she wouldn't be able to keep anything down.

The last weekend I was with Mom, she was ready to die. There weren't any important things left for us to discuss, so she asked me to read to her. Just before I left, I went back into her room to say good-bye one more time. I had a feeling it would be our last time. But there wasn't anything we still needed to say to each other. When she passed away, we had said everything.

After Mom's death there was a huge void for at least six months. I really missed our wonderful times together and having the opportunity to talk with her. The weekends were especially hard because that's when we visited her. Sometimes on a Friday evening, I still think we should get in our car and drive to Philadelphia. That big void is beginning to fade, and now there's a feeling of her presence — little magical things happening in our lives. I believe she's looking out for us.

Since Mom was first diagnosed, Emily and I have been going through a search to become more spiritually grounded: What are our beliefs? What is the afterlife? We started going to church more. My mother had been a missionary, so we always grew up with the church around us — "church" as an institution versus something that was driving our inner selves. The way Mom went so peacefully, we knew she had gone to a better place, some kind of an afterlife. All that energy wasn't going into the ground. Earlier, that kind of idea would have been almost incomprehensible for us, something we had never explored.

My mother showed us that we're only here on this earth for a short time and we should live with gusto while we're here. Getting in touch with that concept has been helpful. Now we're learning to pray. Sometimes we talk to Mom in our prayers. The more we get in touch with our own spirituality, the more we feel her presence.

In the eighteen months of Mom's illness, many people emerged who had been involved with her in the past. As Mom drew closer to her death, she started whittling the numbers down to only a few people she wanted to spend time with, those with positive energy. It became a small group of people, and Joy was one of them. In the past we had often heard Mom talking about her special friend who was going to share a house with her when they retired someday.

After Mom died, we went through a phase of silent mourning, and we didn't talk about her death. Everyone was in their own corner licking their wounds and trying to cope. We had scattered to the winds, and we didn't take time to reminisce and talk about the fun times with her — something we needed to do. When Joy came over after her death, we talked about the good times, the bad times, the funny times, the laughs. It's been very healing to share stories with each other.

We've been amazed at how Mom's presence seems to be around when Joy visits with us, almost filling the room. It's great knowing they went through many similar experiences.

My mother was an astonishing woman who blazed her own trail. She raised us in a very diverse environment and gave each of her sons a sense of independence. The greatest gift she gave me was to believe in myself. Mom knew what was important in life: people and relationships, spirituality, a good education, travel, exploring things, having respect toward all people.

When Emily and I found out we were pregnant, we felt Mom's spirit around us. She probably had a role in helping catch a little soul and bringing it to us. We're sad that Mom won't be around for our children. She would have been the best grandma. She was such a great backer of Emily and me; we couldn't have had a better cheerleader. My mother loved Emily and took her on as her own daughter. As we start our family and live fully in this world, the values and principles Mom believed in have come back to us. We realize that what she was about will live on in what we do.

Before she died, Emily and I asked Mom if there were any words of wisdom she wanted to share with us. She told us, "Love each other." It was so simple, so grounding. That was all we had to know. Mom was a woman who really knew how to love.

The recognition that the world is sacred is one of the most empowering of the many realizations that may occur to people with life-threatening illness. . . . It is one of the ways that such people heal the community around them. And should they die, it is often the legacy they leave behind.

— Rachel Naomi Remen

Goldy's uplifting story illustrates how a strong will, faith, spirituality and love of life can help a person do more than just cope through the pain, adversities and obstacles of a terminal illness and death. Until we die, we can be deeply involved with life and open to new possibilities, new meaning. And, like Goldy, we might even transform death into an opportunity for growth, humor, forgiveness and meaning.

Goldy's thoughts about how to die peacefully are full of excellent suggestions for people facing death (which is every one of us) as well as for families, friends, partners and caregivers. As Goldy discovered, a life-threatening illness can enrich our lives and those of our family and friends.

The day before Goldy died, we spoke on the phone. She was very tired. We did a quick review: She had resolved conflicts and unfinished business, she was surrounded by loving family and friends, her spiritual life was in good order and she had said good-bye to everyone. She felt a genuine sense of satisfaction that she had lived a full life. She was ready to die. Just before we hung up for the last time, she let out a chuckle: "When I get there, Joy, I'll be sure to save you a room with a view — and a rocking chair on the porch." That night my friend died peacefully in her sleep.

But the story didn't end with Goldy's death. Like the grapefruit trees, her legacy of love spins on and on. Although I barely knew her son Andy and his wife Emily, after her death we began getting together to share memories about our much-loved Goldy. Sometimes when I'm with them it feels like Goldy is there too. Occasionally I look around to see if she is. I'm sure she enjoys watching us delight in her sacred legacy.

JOY

Tower of Healing

There is always the possibility that my brain tumor could return.
But for me the more important outcome of this and my two other
close encounters with death is that I have chosen to heal
for my life and for my death. – Joy

Several years ago, I was forced to face the truth that what I had assumed was my strong and lasting grip on life was actually very fragile and fleeting. Three close encounters with death in a three-year period bolted into my life like a stampede of bad nightmares. My initial reactions to these threats to my existence ranged from denial to panic.

During the first round, I contracted a lethal streptococcus infection on my knee, the kind that can quickly take a person's life. I shrugged off that rendezvous with death as though it was merely a bad cold, barely pausing to consider the preciousness of each day or my vulnerability as an earth dweller.

In the second round, as a pedestrian, I was struck by an out-of-control car and thrown through a plate glass window. Since I was nearly killed in the accident, it was difficult to ignore that event. I came to realize that life was not to be taken for granted, nor was it my rightful or merited possession. I began noticing and appreciating the spiritual and emotional qualities of my existence.

The third round finally got my full attention. The diagnosis of a brain tumor brought my fast-track existence to a slower pace and changed my life.

Eventually I came to regard those three exposures to the prospect of death in positive ways. There is no doubt that they served as significant wake-up calls alerting me to the fact that, even though healthy, I was and always will be living close to the edge. I realized that I needed to appreciate the miracle and meaning of my existence in the universe. Together, these experiences changed the way I view the world and enriched the way I live every day. They transformed my former style of existing as a future-oriented, globetrotting, high-pressured executive to one of consciously choosing to live intentionally in the present moment and to pay attention to my body and soul. I now make time for God, people, the wonders of the world, and meaningful work and play. And I'm becoming a more compassionate person.

Looking back, I can understand how my life experiences — my upbringing on a small farm deeply connected to the powerful cycles of nature, numerous interactions with supportive and empowering people, and stimulating work over the years — helped prepare me to heal from life-threatening experiences and to make a fresh start.

Joy

My story begins right smack in the middle of the United States, where everything felt wide open and freeing. I was constantly reminded that the universe is an awesome place to live and we are a tiny part of the great cycle of life. Just outside the little Nebraska town of Clatonia, with its 199 people, my parents, Wilson Julius and Alma Johanna Haupt, raised my sister Shirley and me on what I thought was a magical farm. It was filled with the wonders of haystacks, little lambs with wiggling tails, mulberry trees, bull snakes, coyotes, fuzzy caterpillars, and my dog Brownie.

My mother and father were generous, hard-working, wise people. I don't believe there was a lazy or evil bone in either one of them. My father had such a respect for nature that he never plowed under the 20 acres of original prairie grass that had been growing in that place since the days when the Sioux Indians roamed the Plains. Daddy could have planted some high-producing cash crop on those acres, but he said the prairie was there long before we arrived, and he wanted to preserve it the way it had been so future generations could enjoy it too.

As I grew up, I came to share that reverence for nature and its cycles. Birth and death were normal parts of life as we watched cows, sheep, chickens and pigs give birth and die or be sent off to market to be slaughtered. At funerals for neighbors and relatives, it was natural for children as well as adults to be in attendance. After all, we knew that everyone would die — Grandpa, the piano teacher, the owner of Johnny's Café. The meaning of faith and hope were affirmed each year when Daddy planted the fragile winter wheat seeds just before the harsh cold fronts arrived. Then in the spring we watched the miraculous transformation of the fields as they came alive with the brilliant green sprouts of that tough wheat.

Over time, I inherited some of my parents' qualities, particularly their passionate interest in helping people and animals. Even as a small child, if I saw other beings hurt, I wanted to help them. When my dog Brownie had his leg cut off in a hay mowing accident, I spent hours petting and hugging him, trying to help him heal. After I witnessed a terrible barn fire and heard the pitiful screams of the horses and cows trapped inside, I vowed I would make the world a safer place — for people and animals.

Although as a child I thought of myself as the heroic helper and healer, my folks must have thought I was a daydreamer, especially when they gave me a simple task like bringing home the cows to be milked. On the way to the pasture, I passed barbed wire fences strung between interesting fence posts made from dead tree branches. To me, each one of those fence posts was a potential friend, and some of them were in pretty bad shape. For example, "Sandy" had two stubby branches sticking out the top of her "head." I imagined the poor thing was either a freak in the circus or a cousin of the devil. "Susie" was terribly bent and misshapen, perhaps from an accident or a birth defect. Whatever had happened, I tried to provide sympathy and attention to my fence post friends. It's not surprising that as a child I dreamed of being a doctor when I grew up.

As the seasons passed, mega-farming began to appear on the horizon, with its expensive high-tech equipment and enormous debts. My father saw the writing on the wall: It would be difficult to remain a small farmer without any sons in the family, and my mother had already developed some hefty allergies and asthma. I earnestly promised him I would stay on the farm and help him forever. After all, I was a terrific cow milker, and I had been driving the tractor since I was big enough to reach the clutch.

But in the end, Daddy was right, and when I was thirteen we sold our beloved farm and moved to Lincoln. Initially that move was a frightening experience. There were so many new people, and I had to go to a huge school where we studied weird things like geometry and French and no one wore hand-me-down clothes.

A few years later when I entered Nebraska Wesleyan University, my advisors informed me that only a paltry number of women were being accepted into medical school in Nebraska. They strongly encouraged me to consider another, more appropriate profession for a woman. Of course, not having ever heard the words "equal opportunity," I relinquished my dream of medicine and yielded to their suggestion of pursuing the acceptable route of becoming a schoolteacher.

After graduation I moved to Southern California to the land of sunshine, orange groves and eucalyptus trees, where I taught in an affluent elementary school. A colleague teacher down the hall seemed determined not to allow me to get too comfortable. She constantly bugged me about my bourgeois life and challenged me to reach out to those less fortunate than our middle-class students. Because of her tenacity, I eventually signed up as a volunteer, teaching English to Mexican migrant workers two evenings a week.

Even though my ten students lived and worked in miserable conditions, their zest for life was palpable, and their gratitude for the opportunity to learn English touched my soul. That volunteer experience encouraged me to apply for a teaching position on a Navajo reservation.

But I never made it there. Before the contract arrived, I met Marguerite, a dynamic woman who had worked for years as a missionary in China. She talked about the problems and desperate needs of poor people in developing countries, and I found myself drawn to the possibility of responding to such a challenge. Months later, after filling out endless papers, I was at graduate school preparing for my new life in Asia.

However, nothing could totally prepare me for my first international work in the slums of Karachi, West Pakistan. In mud hut homes, which often washed away during monsoon seasons, I saw poverty and disease that I had never imagined. And I witnessed firsthand the helplessness of women whose lives had almost no worth within their society. Men joked about valuing their children, their belongings, and their goats more than their wives. Many women were abandoned or divorced if they didn't bear sons, and often the parents of those rejected women were unwilling to take their shamed daughters back into their homes again.

Yet in the midst of misery and wretchedness in some of the worst slums of Karachi, I experienced a great deal of sharing and happiness. Although the children in the one-room mud schoolhouses had no desks or books and sat on gunnysacks on dirt floors, they seemed more enthusiastic about learning than we had been in my comparatively affluent one-room schoolhouse in Nebraska. In over 100-degree weather, surrounded by open sewers with flies and mosquitoes swarming around, families welcomed me into their tiny homes. There we sat on the dirt floor and talked and laughed together as we shared a precious cup of tea, which we passed around drinking from it until it was empty. I was often amazed to see contentment and joy in the eyes of those poorest of the poor.

Drinking tea from a shared cup and working in the slums of Karachi, however, did have risks. Toward the end of my three years, I became very ill with ailments like dengue fever, amoebic hepatitis and malaria. I was forced to be completely bedridden for nearly three months, and for the first time I experienced frustration and disappointment and what it meant to be seriously ill. I began to understand how easy it would be to lose one's optimism and patience, and even one's faith in the possibility of healing.

When I recovered, I returned to the United States to re-embark on my teaching and counseling career, eventually winning the award for the Outstanding Young Educator of the United States. I became involved in the creation of community projects in New York City, including a storefront neighborhood assistance program, a project for teenagers at risk and a women's training and counseling center.

Soon doors started opening to many other interesting international work-related opportunities with the Ford Foundation, Church World Service, the United Nations, Save the Children, and the Christian Children's Fund. Along with these exciting opportunities came some tough and ferocious illnesses.

When I worked for Save the Children as the Director of the Asia/ Pacific Region, I traveled extensively, becoming familiar with nearly every airport in the region. On one of my trips to Sri Lanka I contracted a lethal streptococcus infection on my left knee. Fortunately, I was already flying back to the United States when it hit me. Within hours after landing, my knee had swollen to the size of a bright amber football and I couldn't walk on my left leg without excruciating pain. As soon as the doctor saw me, he sent me directly to the hospital and began intravenous antibiotics. He called in top-notch doctors to help with the diagnosis and treatment. The infection rapidly progressed into scarlet fever as my temperature hovered around 105 degrees. For several days, the doctors battled my scorching fever and the infection as I lay on ice packs, while massive dosages of antibiotics flowed into my body. They nervously watched the red streaks traveling up my leg and abdomen, afraid that the infection would reach my heart and kill me.

But I was oblivious to the dangers as I continued to make phone calls to check on the progress of various Save the Children projects. When the nurses came to restart my intravenous fluids, which tended to make me nauseated, I sometimes asked if they could hold off for a few minutes so I could finish my international calls. Eventually the right medication and excellent treatment by my nurses and doctors arrested the infection and saved my life, probably just in the nick of time. However, I was too busy to think much about that experience. As soon as I could walk with a cane, I went back to my work and its hectic schedule.

A year later on a "ten plus" summer day filled with bright sunshine, a royal blue sky and a cool breeze, I was standing on the sidewalk of a quiet cul-de-sac street in Greenport, Long Island, waiting for my friends who were poking around the charming shops near the marina. I had decided not to go shopping and was enjoying the superb weather as I waited for them in front of Preston's Store. The only thing on my mind was what we would have for dinner that night.

Just as I was contemplating fresh fish and corn on the cob, a woman backed her car out of a parking space across the street and stomped on the accelerator instead of the brake. Rolling across the street like a bowling ball, her car struck me and knocked down a heavy four-by-four pole holding up the roof over the sidewalk. The pole hit me on the right side of my head. Then the car, the pole and I crashed into the window of Preston's Store, shattering the plate glass. I was knocked unconscious with a fractured skull and serious lacerations and injuries to my head, neck and back. Without a doubt, I had been in the wrong place at the wrong time.

Because I was immediately knocked out, I have no memory of anything related to the accident itself. But I do recall trying to open my heavy eyes and realizing a stranger was kneeling beside me in the glass. Because the sunlight was behind her bushy hair, it looked like she had a halo. She sounded like a broken record as she told me over and over how important it was for me to stay awake. Although I wanted desperately to close my eyes and sleep, she somehow convinced me not to do that.

After what seemed a long time, an ambulance arrived and paramedics began checking my vital signs. Noting skull-deep cuts, the swelling of my head, the loss of blood and my dilating eyes, they were concerned that I was slipping into a coma.

Throughout the entire process, the stranger, who told me her name was Rosemary, stayed by my side and held my hand as she gently encouraged me to hang on a little longer. She constantly reassured me that I would be okay. Through her strength and concern, this guardian angel spun a protective cocoon around me, blocking out much of the trauma and fear that an accident victim usually experiences.

When the paramedics lifted me into the ambulance and Rosemary momentarily let go of my hands, I felt the first wave of panic rush through me. I had lost the lifeline to my angel, and I felt alone and afraid. Through my oxygen mask I tried to talk to the young woman taking my blood pressure in the ambulance, but my tongue felt thick and the words came out garbled. She smiled and patted my hand, "Don't worry, honey. Your friend will be right back. She's talking to the police."

Just before the ambulance doors were closed for the ride to the nearest hospital, Rosemary jumped in and resumed her post at my side. When she was certain that I was safely in the hands of the emergency room staff, she left me and returned to the scene of the accident where she found my friends. By then they were worried about my absence at the designated meeting place and suspected that I might have been the victim at the site of the terrible accident in front of Preston's.

Finally, late at night after promising to call me the next day, my angel left. Doctors have told me that the presence of Rosemary probably kept me from slipping into a dangerous coma. She may have saved my life.

After being knocked unconscious, with a fractured skull, injuries to my cervical spine, body-wide bruises and lacerations, stitches, neck and back pains, headaches and post traumatic stress syndrome with recurring nightmares, it may sound a bit like Pollyanna for me to say "I was lucky." But I was. Early on, the x-rays showed that I was having cerebral hemorrhaging. The doctors were concerned that I might develop blood clots on my brain, which could result in seizures, strokes or other problems. But with physical therapy and exercise I totally recovered.

Perhaps one of the best outcomes from the accident was my new friendship with my guardian angel Rosemary. I have great admiration and respect for this courageous woman who could have decided, as many people would have, not to get involved with a stranger who was bleeding and unconscious. But she chose to kneel on the carpet of shattered glass and reach out to me.

A year later I received another astonishing gift from this strange encounter with death. I had moved to Richmond, Virginia, to become Director of International Programs for the Christian Children's Fund. After a routine brain scan as a follow-up to the accident, I was shocked when the doctor turned from the x-rays hanging on the wall and said, "You have a brain tumor. It must be removed as soon as possible." It felt like the blood in my veins turned icy cold. It just couldn't be true; the doctor wasn't really talking about me. I was healthy, energetic and full of life. "Are you sure?" was all I could say.

"Yes, it's definitely a brain tumor. Have you had any seizures, headaches or loss of eyesight? The tumor is located in a key area of your brain." The doctor began talking about the risks of surgery: "There's a five to ten percent chance of death during the surgical procedures, a five to ten percent chance of your being in a coma, a five to ten percent chance of your bleeding to death if I accidentally cut the major vein the tumor rests on, a five to ten percent chance of partial paralysis, a five to ten percent chance of loss of speech or loss of the use of your right arm and leg, . . ." As he continued, I frantically tried to add up what felt like a lot of five to ten percent risks. My disoriented arithmetic came up with a sum around 100 percent.

In less than a minute, my entire world had been turned upside down. I felt devastated that my life was totally out of control, perhaps never to be in place again. Panic choked me as I realized I might die if they performed the surgery, and I would certainly die if they didn't. I felt so frightened that I considered taking my chances and doing nothing. I was in total denial.

After leaving the doctor's office, I have no recollection of driving to Second Presbyterian Church where I had planned to attend a prayer service that evening. It was already in progress when I walked into the chapel. I opened the hymnbook, but the words looked blurred and the prayers seemed to be in a strange language.

At the end of the service, with a lump in my throat, I told Kerry Pidcock-Lester, one of the ministers, my awful news. "I have a brain tumor." Wrapped in the security of her empathy, I could admit to her how scared I was. I asked her to pray for me but not to mention my name to anyone. I was afraid there might be a stigma attached to having a brain tumor. Taking my hands, she prayed, "God, sometimes our burdens seem almost too much for us to bear. This one feels very heavy for Joy." With those simple words, my defenses broke down, and my bottled-up tears burst from my eyes, splashing our entwined fingers. Kerry gently suggested I might consider asking others for support.

The next day I tested her suggestion and phoned several church members. To my surprise they seemed pleased that I had reached out to them, and they wanted to help. Later that week Kerry and I mapped a strategy that would provide maximum support and strength for my emotional and spiritual needs in the days ahead. We discussed the possibility of having a special healing service after Evening Prayer the following week. Although I had never experienced one, it seemed like a good idea.

In the meantime, I contacted family and friends and asked them to help me in my preparations for healing. I also took this opportunity to tell them how much I loved them, forgiving them and asking for their forgiveness when necessary. I spent hours reading the scriptures and inspirational books on healing. I prayed alone and with friends asking for guidance, acceptance, peace of mind and healing. I went on a brief silent retreat.

Fortunately, I was able to find a very supportive neurosurgeon, Dr. Harold F. Young, the Chief Neurosurgeon at the Medical Colleges of Virginia Hospital. Not only was he highly skilled and respected, he also made me feel part of a team that would help me get well. The first time I met Dr. Young, we spent a few minutes getting acquainted with each other. After he sensed I was feeling comfortable, he asked, "Joy, shall we take a look at the x-rays?" He didn't say, "Now I'll take a look at your x-rays." I felt he valued my opinion, and I immediately wanted to participate in the decision-making process.

When I asked Dr. Young about the risks for surgery, he paused for a minute before he answered: "You are healthy, you love life. I think there are almost no risks for you because *you will be very involved with your own healing process.*" By saying those crucial words to me, he validated my having a major role in my own healing. I was not just a passive recipient of his medical treatment.

Leaving Dr. Young's office, I went directly to the blood bank to give blood should it be needed during my surgery. I felt a new sense of confidence. I canceled activities on my calendar that appeared stressful or not useful to my preparation. I gathered and read as much information about brain tumors as I could absorb. I tried out different kinds of healing processes to complement the traditional Western medical procedures, including massage therapy, a superb nutritional diet, herbal teas and exercise. I meditated and imaged positive outcomes.

My friend Mary Ann taught me how to use imagery as a healing tool. I thought of my tumor as a gladiola bulb, which needed to shrink so it could easily be removed from my head and taken to a place where gladiolas bloom — definitely not in my brain. Three times a day I sat quietly and imagined myself wrapping and tying my "gladiola bulb" with blue light to shrink it. I ended each session by spreading gold light on my brain to help it heal. After my surgery Dr. Young said that when they opened my skull, my tumor was quite easy to remove. Perhaps the steroids I took the week before surgery did a lot of the work, but I believe the imagery and positive thoughts helped too.

Usually I'm a very active and lively person, and I always have one more thing I want to do, so it has always been difficult for me to slow down. But the brain tumor forced me to realize I was near the edge of a cliff. It was important to stop and enjoy life in whatever time I had left. Every hour might have been my last chance to be kind and loving to myself and to others. So I spent time with my family and friends, listened to peaceful music, watched sunrises and sunsets, looked at my favorite scenery and stopped to smell the flowers. This, too, was how I was involved in my own healing.

With only six days left before my surgery, I returned to church for the special healing service. About 30 people had gathered in the chapel. Ben Sparks, one of the ministers, began. "Friends, God knows our needs before we ask, and in our asking prepares us to receive the gift of grace. Let us open our lives to God's healing presence." As the words of Romans 8:38 were read, I began to feel a warm, soothing peace flowing over me in contrast to the earlier uncontrollable fear.

> *For I am convinced that neither death nor life, nor*
> *anything else in all creation, will be able to separate us*
> *from the love of God.*

My friends gathered around and reached out to lay their hands on me. As their hands pressed down, I was surprised that it felt like a weight almost too heavy to bear was being placed on me. But inside my head I heard these words: "Be open, Joy. Flow with the feeling of this heavy weight, feel this connectedness, feel the need for healing."

Suddenly I was aware of the warmth of the earth beneath my knees — almost hugging me to its healing power. And I knew I was not alone, but connected to every person whose hands were on me. We all needed healing in some way: physically, mentally, spiritually, socially. And we were all dying. We were carrying our woundedness, our brokenness, like massive yokes around our necks. By touching one another from the tenderness of our hearts and joining our human needs, we could share the power of healing love.

As I stood up and hugged everyone, I saw that each one of us had tears flowing down our faces. Perhaps they were washing and cleansing the wounds and fears in our hearts. When I left the chapel that night, I knew the tumor was still inside my head but a lot of healing had already taken place.

The day before surgery I felt relaxed enough to enjoy a drive through the beautiful Blue Ridge Mountains with my father and sister, who had arrived from California. Together we reviewed our life stories and the richness of our family ties. We went to my attorney's office to witness my living will. That evening we ate a light dinner with friends. Dr. Young called to reassure me that he had been reviewing my x-rays and everything looked good for surgery the next morning.

Later that night my father, sister and I prayed together, and as Shirley gently brushed my hair, Daddy read and reread the 23rd Psalm:

Though I walk through the valley of the shadow of death,
I will fear no evil, for Thou art with me.

It was dark and cold when we took a taxi to the hospital the next morning. At 6:00 A.M., Ben joined us in the Admitting Office to pray with us. Just before I left for surgery, Daddy told me how proud he and my mother were of my work and how much they loved me. I felt very cherished, appreciated and calm as I said good-bye to my father and sister. When the orderly took me into the operating room, I no longer experienced the bone-chilling fear I had when I first learned of my tumor. Although I was keenly aware that I could die or be seriously disabled, I was prepared for that or for a complete recovery. I knew my work had been successful; I was already healed and at peace.

Before I was put to sleep, I told the doctors, "I've done my homework, now I'm in God's and your hands." The last thing I remember saying was, "While I'm asleep, please tell me that I'm doing great. I'll hear you, and it will help my recovery." They promised to do so.

Seven hours later, just before 1:00 P.M., my skull was closed and a turban-like bandage wrapped around my head. I woke up in the Intensive Care Unit able to see clearly the clock on the wall. I told the nurses who were connecting me to the monitors surrounding my bed, "It's already ten minutes after one. So when will they do the surgery?" They looked surprised at my alertness. When I was told the surgery was already completed, I suddenly realized I was able to speak, I could move my arms and legs without any difficulty, I wasn't in a coma and I wasn't paralyzed. I was certainly alive! I was so ecstatic about this wonderful outcome that whenever people passed my bed I told them, "I'm so happy. Thank God, I'm okay. I'm so happy!" Later one of the nurses told my sister they had never seen a patient come out of seven hours of brain surgery so wide awake and coherent.

Less than 18 hours after surgery, I was out of the Intensive Care Unit and placed in a regular room in the hospital. A few hours later I called my mother in California before taking my first walk down the hallway to the nurses' station. Just four days after surgery, I had made so much progress that Dr. Young discharged me from the hospital.

Only three weeks after I first heard the dreadful news of my brain tumor, I was back in church for the weekly Prayer Service. The chapel had never looked so beautiful. I had not remembered the light shining through the stained glass windows in quite that way. The pianist played peaceful music that gently took me to green pastures and still waters, and the faces of my friends appeared to glow with a new radiance. When Kerry read the words of the scriptures, they seemed written for me.

It's been several years now since that surgery, and follow-up tests have shown no sign of the tumor. There is always the possibility that it could return. But for me the more important outcome of this and the two earlier experiences is that I have healed for my life and for my death.

Healing, like prayer, is the transmission of energy and the emanation of spiritual light. It is not meant as a cure for disease, but as an aid in assisting you toward your destiny.
— Shoni Labowitz

Tremendous growth can come from the process I now call "healing for meaningful living and for peaceful dying." All of us live with the possibility of death, of course, but many of us don't pay much attention to it. Then along comes an accident or illness or tragedy, and we realize that we need to make some changes before it is too late.

Three close encounters with death taught me to be more appreciative of each moment and to be grateful for every gift of life. These health crises showed me what I was made of as I faced my fears and called upon my strengths. After these wakeup calls, I made a conscious decision to slow down and make time for my spirituality and for the activities and people that enrich my life. This was not a new direction for me, just a shift in emphasis. Growth often comes that way.

I have always been quite self-reliant, since my days of finding friends in those Nebraska fence posts. In my career, I have been a take-charge self-starter, usually operating at full steam. So I was a good candidate for the challenge given me: to be involved in my healing process. But I also chose to take concrete steps — things anybody can do — to make myself a more fertile garden for both the medical treatments and the nurturing care that were essential for my survival.

Although I required top-of-the line medical care, I also needed the emotional, social and spiritual support of my family, friends and church. And I put my ultimate faith in God. In the end I was able to relax and let go, knowing I had done everything possible to help.

Since these experiences I began listening to others who had also faced crises. I discovered again and again one simple truth: Whereas we might not be able to cure ourselves, we can choose to help heal ourselves, no matter what challenge we are facing.

Hope begins in the dark,
the stubborn hope that if you just show up
and try to do the right thing,
the dawn will come.
You wait and watch and work;
you don't give up.

– Anne Lamott

We have only begun
to imagine the fullness of life.
How could we tire of hope?
So much is in the bud.

– Denise Levertov

Afterword

Healing is one of the most ancient and important services that human beings can give each other. – Richard Katz

In a world filled with threats of terrorism and war, economic and job instability, anxiety and loss, it is not surprising that we can be shaken to our very core. Indeed, we may sometimes feel hopeless — almost trapped in grief, pain and fear.

These Towers of Hope stories have clearly shown that suffering and adversity can also serve in another capacity. They have the potential to change the picture for us, to transform us, to provide a way for us to find significance and meaning in our lives. In the very worst of times, we may discover some surprising gifts that have been buried in the ashes of life: compassion, the desire to serve, wisdom, fresh understandings, courage, hope and healing.

The people in this book have provided us some worthy illustrations of how we can choose not to concentrate all of our concerns on what is painful or frightening. Although their tribulations were extremely troublesome and required close attention, they did not make their woundedness the central focus of their existence. If they had, they may have become hostages to an endless process of anger, skepticism, fear, bitterness and self-pity. Rather, they chose to transform their lives and make them more meaningful and worthwhile. In the process they found hope and healing.

How Do We Heal?

There is no single road to wellness. Getting well and being well is taking an interlocking network of highways that lead to the one, central junction of wholeness.

                – John Robert McFarland

As I listen to people tell their stories of healing, I am astonished by the numerous and diverse ways that we can be "healed." Although some of us may appear to be more open to healing because of our personality type or genetic disposition, there is not one single path to wholeness or wellness. Every one of us heals in our own way and under different kinds of conditions. Nevertheless, there are some common themes or threads that I have found repeatedly woven throughout healing stories.

We can take these themes and turn them into questions for ourselves. We may find such questions a bit tough or challenging, and most likely they will not provide us with easy or pat answers. But they may act as guideposts to help us face our problems and our needs for healing with greater clarity, understanding and openness. In the process we might discover opportunities to become more alive, more courageous and hopeful, more healed.

- ## Do I have a desire and a willingness to heal?
  Having the desire or aspiration to heal, to be whole, is an important component in the healing process. For some of us, that may translate as approaching our problems or woundedness with a positive attitude.

Even when we can't modify our situation, we can still change our attitude. If we do, there is a strong possibility that our lives will improve. For others, it may mean approaching healing from a more contemplative attitude — of going deeply into and even beneath our problems. Here at "Ground Zero" we may find meaning and hope that lie well beneath the surface, beyond our capacity to effect a positive outcome. In the silence, we may experience the mystery of our reality and may find courage to respond favorably and positively to our predicament. Perhaps we, and the situation, will be transformed. As the *Tao Te Ching* points out: new possibilities may present themselves to us "when the mud settles."

- ## Do I have an open heart?
  In the midst of hardship, it is important to cultivate an open heart. An open heart is an unveiled heart, an enlightened heart, a humane heart, a grateful heart, a listening heart, an embracing heart, a heart that can savor passion and pain. When our hearts have been "broken open," we will likely feel immense amounts of suffering and sadness. We may also experience a genuine empathy for the problems of the world. An unguarded heart can soften us and make us more compassionate. In the process we may reap a bounty of love, generosity, joy and satisfaction.

- ## Am I willing to forgive myself?
  Some of the most profound healing occurs if we are willing to admit and embrace our shadow sides and our fragmentation, to pull together our good, our mediocre and our bad pieces. When we learn how to practice genuine self-forgiveness and reconciliation with our limitations, we will likely experience self-acceptance. That's when we can begin to sense our "wholeness" and authenticity.

- ## Can I forgive others?
  Although often difficult, forgiving others is an important ingredient in the healing process. By forgiving, we are able to free ourselves of resentments, fear and anger, resistance to change, toxic poisons in our bodies and minds, even our self-imposed isolation. At that point, some greater generosity takes over, and life may become fuller and more fruitful.

- ## Do I have a spiritual life?

  Generally, our lives will feel richer and we will reap positive benefits when we have a deep and meaningful spiritual life or a relationship with the Divine. Connecting to a higher power or perspective often brings calmness, well being, and a sense of peace and healing. It may also give us the courage and strength to reach out with compassion to our friends and enemies as well as to those who are suffering.

- ## Do I want to serve others?

  Healing often occurs when we reach out with real compassion and generosity to help others. Mercy and kindness toward others have the power to almost miraculously heal some of our own neediness and deprivation. This seems to be especially true when we are involved in rectifying social and political injustices.

- ## Am I open to change and to new ways of experiencing life?

  Being open to our dilemmas and turning a tough situation into a challenge or an advantage can be enriching. and we may be able to bring forth what is good within ourselves. When crises and problems are viewed as an opportunity rather than a moral judgment or condemnation, we create a more hospitable environment for healing.

- ## Am I willing to face reality?

  Unfortunately most problems don't get totally solved, and improving things is done in small, incremental steps. Healing can be enhanced when we have a willingness to face life for what it is — both the good and the bad sides — and to allow room for misery and joy, anguish and relief.

- ## Can I find the courage to face tough times, trauma, even death?

  Despair, loss, grief and the possibility of death can act like powerful messengers assisting us to pay attention to what is really going on with our lives, to what is truly important and valuable. Sometimes we are forced to stop hiding from our true selves or escaping into the future or distorting the past. By confronting trauma and life-threatening illnesses, we can break through to a more essential understanding of ourselves and of life itself. It can also help us recognize what has real meaning, enabling us to live more fully in the present moment and enjoy each day, even when the options of life seem more limited than they once did.

- ## Can I let go of negative thoughts and memories?
Negativity begets negativity. And negative, judgmental thoughts and memories act as poisonous toxins that inhibit healing. By not dwelling on our "misery" and releasing its controlling patterns, we may find ourselves in an improved situation.

- ## Do I have support systems in my life?
We all need support and encouragement. Having a place to safely unload our burdens of anxiety and frustration, without the fear of being judged, is particularly valuable. There is a kind of natural healing that takes place when supportive family and friends reassure and comfort us. Having a sense of belonging in a community can be empowering and uplifting.

- ## Do I find delight in life?
If we have an openness to the wonder, beauty and splendor that are around us in nature, in friendship, in love, in meaningful activities, in ordinary things, we will likely be more open to the mystery and gift of "healing."

- ## Am I able to be patient with myself and others?
Being patient does not mean "enduring" or "grinning and bearing it" or playing a sacrificial role. When we are patient, we can be more gentle and honest with ourselves and with others. Patience can help us to be more open and accepting of whatever comes our way. It can serve as a type of antidote to depression, anger and self-pity.

- ## Do I take care of myself?
Taking proper care of our bodies, minds and emotions can be an accelerator of the healing process. This can include many forms: appropriate nutrition and exercise, adequate rest, stress-reducing

relaxation and meditation techniques, imagery and visualization exercises, prayer and spiritual practices, retreats.

It can be said that whatever occurs can be regarded as the path and that all things, not just some things, are workable. This teaching is a fearless proclamation of what's possible for ordinary people like you and me.

– Pema Chodron

These are difficult times in which we live. We have learned to accept that darkness, heartache, agony and insecurity will always be a part of the panorama of life. But we have also come to realize that even when we are about to give up, when we feel no motivation or inspiration, even then we can experience healing in our pain.

These Towers of Hope stories have provided us many inspiring lessons that can restore us and fill us with courage and hope. Through their vivid examples, they have passed on to us heartening "instructions" on how we too can encounter "healing" along our uncertain paths. They verify that we can find treasures even when we are in the abyss of suffering.

Having invited you into the world of these hope-filled, healing stories, I now invite you to join me in planting new seeds of hope in the universe, in the ashes and landscape of life, by passing on our own stories of healing. Perhaps we can step into fresh territory as we watch our seeds sprout and grow into strong saplings reaching for the sky with optimism and perseverance — like Towers of Hope.

Joy Carol is an author, spiritual director, counselor and guest speaker at conferences. She leads retreats and workshops on spirituality, healing, avoiding burnout, death and dying, and compassionate caregiving at medical schools, seminaries, retreat centers, churches and other groups. She is on the healing ministry at the St. Luke's School of Healing and at the Cathedral of St. John the Divine in New York City. Over the last 25 years, she has been a writer, psychological counselor, educator (the Outstanding Young Educator of the USA) and manager of international development programs. She has lived and worked in the developing world for organizations such as the Ford Foundation, UNDP, Save the Children, and the Christian Children's Fund.

Six years ago Joy had three close encounters with death and has since dedicated her life to spirituality and healing. She holds an honorary doctorate in Humane Letters from Nebraska Wesleyan University, master's degrees in Spiritual Direction from the General Theological Seminary in NYC and in counseling psychology from the University of Maryland. She has also done graduate studies in Asian Affairs, women and development, and management at Scarritt College, New York University and Harvard University. She has been trained and is experienced in hospice work, grief counseling, healing techniques, Reiki, Therapeutic Touch, imagery and meditation.